Dorene Lehavi, MSW, PhD
Business Partnership Essentials

Dorene Lehavi, MSW, PhD

Business Partnership Essentials

A Step-by-Step Action Plan for Succeeding in Business
with a Partner

Second Edition

ISBN 978-1-5474-1617-2
e-ISBN (PDF) 978-1-5474-0018-8
e-ISBN (EPUB) 978-1-5474-0020-1

Library of Congress Cataloging-in-Publication Data
A CIP catalog record for this book has been applied for at the Library of Congress.

Bibliographic information published by the Deutsche Nationalbibliothek
The Deutsche Nationalbibliothek lists this publication in the Deutsche Nationalbibliografie;
detailed bibliographic data are available on the Internet at http://dnb.dnb.de.

© 2018 Dorene Lehavi
Published by Walter de Gruyter Inc., Boston/Berlin
Cover image: baona/iStock/Getty Images Plus
Printing and binding: CPI book GmbH, Leck
♾ Printed on acid-free paper
Printed in Germany

www.degruyter.com

Praise for *Business Partnership Essentials*

In my years of practicing law, I have seen what happens when business partnerships work well. They tend to thrive bringing good things to the partners, and their families, employees, customers, and the community at large. I have also seen what happens when partners find themselves entrenched in a business divorce. Bottom line—there are no winners in a business divorce.

Your book really helped me to get a better understanding of how to put together lasting partnerships, and how to recognize the signs of a failing partnership so that I can be of better assistance in correcting a ship that is headed in the wrong direction. Your book has and will make me a better attorney and counselor.

—Demetri Chambers, Esq.
Walker & Chambers
Attorneys and Counselors at Law

The advice in *Business Partnership Essentials* has real and far-reaching impact, not just on individuals and their businesses but the national economy. Dr. Lehavi has written a five-star book. I suggest you run–don't walk–to get your copy.

—Dr. Paula Fellingham
Founder, The Women's Information Network
TheWINonline.com

Other books on business partnerships may agree that choosing the right partner is crucial, but Dr. Lehavi actually shares how to do it. She covers every detail–including things that are not commonly known or done–and does it in plain language that any business owner can understand. Whether you're looking to form a business partnership or create a joint venture, this book has you covered.

—Sandra Martini
ExtremeClientCare.com

Dr. Lehavi is boldly helping to reverse the 70% business partnership failure rate in the United States. Very few people have thought about this very important matter as much as Dr. Lehavi. Considering that your business partner is perhaps the most important factor to your business's success, this book is paramount to selecting and nurturing your relationship with your business partner.

—Shahab Kaviani
Co-founder, CoFoundersLab (a Onevest Company)

If you are in a partnership or considering one, read this book. Partnerships form the backbone of business, yet few people are properly educated on what makes them effective, fulfilling and profitable. In a readable, down-to-earth manner, Dr. Lehavi shares her wealth of practical knowledge about partnerships that work.

—Hal Goldstein
Founder and partner, iPhone Life Magazine and Usedhandhelds.com
Author of *The Meditating Entrepreneurs: Creating Success from the Inside Out*

This step-by-step guide to setting up a business partnership will help you see the red flags and avoid common traps that most partnerships fall into.

—Liat Cohen, Esq.
Alperstein, Simon, Farkas, Gillin & Scott, LLP

I've seen too many entrepreneurs and startups waste precious energy with partner in-fighting. Dr. Lehavi lays out a path that allows founders to focus on growing their businesses rather than solving personality conflicts. A must–read for startups with multiple founders.

—Eric P. Rose, NPDP, MBA
Product Innovation and Management Consultant
Professor of Entrepreneurship,
Loyola Marymount University

Dr. Lehavi expands your vision, focus and confidence with thoughtful, sound counsel. Her guidance is as comfortable as it is valuable and it generates better, stronger partnerships.

—David Hamlin and Sydney Weisman
Weisman Hamlin Public Relations
Whpr.com

Dr. Lehavi's *pièce de résistance* is her brilliant Business Partnership Agreement Template. Don't go into partnership without it!

—Lynn Holley
Founder and CEO, River Moss Productions
Rivermossproductions.com

Business Partnership Essentials is a strategic platform upon which cofounders and joint venture partners can have a serious, open, ongoing discussion about their plans and expectations. After reading this book, I've found that the actual legal agreement is far less important than the conversations leading up to its drafting.

—Danielle Julia Cuomo, MBA
President, Virtual Assist USA

If your goal is to succeed in business with your partner(s), you must read this book. *Business Partnership Essentials* covers the most important actions that partners need to take—before, during and after startup—in order to lay a solid foundation for non-stop growth.

—CK Wilde
CEO, Customer Rush Marketing

Well-written and accessible, this super tool addresses issues that people don't usually consider when forming a partnership. I discovered some things that I hadn't thought about even though I've been in a successful partnership for 12 years.

—Pauline Raschella
Owner, Raschella Home Decor

To all entrepreneurs, especially those in partnerships, who recognize that business is about relationships on every level.

I honor all of you for your courage, commitment to your dreams, and your contributions to the local and global economy
by providing goods, services and JOBS!

"The only thing that binds people together is the fact that under all circumstances, most people, without knowing what the other will do, will reach for the golden rope of justice, truth, decency and fairness, and thereby bind themselves to every other person who grasps the same rope. This is the only combination that will endure."

–Unknown

Acknowledgments

Many people supported me, with a great deal of patience, throughout the years when this book was just an idea and a goal of mine. I offer my heartfelt thanks to everyone who played a role in this work—including offering me a physical space in which to write, assisting with focus groups and arranging interviews, and giving feedback on the early drafts.

To all the individuals who contributed their stories to the two editions of this book and especially to the successful partnerships who generously gave of their time for interviews: Thank you for sharing your "must haves" to succeed.

I wish to express my gratitude to the A-team who helped put my message into book form: Gina Mazza, cover designer, Lee Ann Fortunato-Heltzel, who worked together with my personal virtual assistant, Danielle Cuomo. Their collaboration with me on this project near to my heart was a partnership in its own right.

Finally, I would like to thank the people at De Gruyter (De|G Press), Jeff Pepper for talking me into the revision, Jaya Dalal and Christopher Link for their edits, and Angie MacAllister and her team for the production work.

DOI 10.1515/9781547400188-201

About the Author

Dr. Dorene Lehavi's professional mission is to reverse the devastating 70% failure rate of business partnerships. Her education, training and experience as a business coach, psychotherapist and relationships expert make her uniquely qualified to rescue partnerships from the brink.

As owner of Business Partner Pro, she coaches entrepreneurs worldwide and has created a series of do-it-yourself tools to help ensure their success. Her *Guide to Choosing the Right Partner*, Business Partnership Agreement Template (BPAT) and *What If Scenario Handbook to Prepare for the Unexpected Before it Occurs* are extremely effective tools for getting partnerships off on the right foot and keeping them on track for the long term.

Dr. Lehavi, a resident of Los Angeles, acquired her MSW at Hunter College in New York City and her PhD from the University of Southern California. In addition to coaching entrepreneurs and partnerships, Dorene is a licensed clinical social worker, who supervises interns and sees private clients. Dr. Lehavi is a board member of The People Concern in Los Angeles, which serves the mentally ill homeless. In addition, she periodically mentors at-risk teens and members of the recovery community, and avidly supports various local and global causes. Dorene is a collage artist, and she enjoys writing and ballroom dancing.

To learn more or to reach Dorene Lehavi, visit www.bizpartnerpro.com.

DOI 10.1515/9781547400188-202

Contents

Civic economic study findings are unequivocal: independent businesses bring substantial benefits to their local economies when compared to large chain store competitors. While chain retailers and restaurants remove locally generated revenues from the community, independent small- and mid-size businesses create a cycle of local spending. These extra dollars in the local economy produce more jobs for residents, extra tax revenues for local governments, more investment in commercial and residential districts, and enhanced support for local nonprofits. In short, these businesses create better places to live. One example: A recent study of Salt Lake City by Utah Civic Economics showed that small businesses return a total of 52% of all revenue to the local economy; and restaurateurs return 78.6%. At the same time, big-box stores like Barnes & Noble, Home Depot, Office Max and Target recirculate an average of 13.6% of all revenue within the local markets that host their stores.

Periods of economic uncertainty can be a time of new opportunity, and entrepreneurs are the ones who are finding ways to transform personal strengths into powerful entrepreneurial endeavors. Think about the plethora of creative ideas and innovations that are present today and you will realize that many of them reveal how people are taking time to discover their passions and put them into action. Have you ever watched the popular reality TV show "Shark Tank", where endless dreamers leave their jobs and professions to open a business to manufacture and sell their innovative products and services? Many of my own clients left lucrative law practices and other careers to open their dream businesses—everything from a florist shop, coffee house and art gallery, to manufacturing home accessories or starting a nonprofit.

As budding entrepreneurs succeed, grow and enrich the market, they also hire other people. The business world is an arena of interaction among people, so relationships are naturally a key factor. When a partnership fails, the cost is not just financial. The 70% of failed partnerships mentioned above also represents the emotional and psychological pain, confusion and losses that result when business relationships go bad. Dissolution of a partnership affects family members, investors, employees, customers, suppliers, the community and, ultimately, the global economy.

The point is this: whether you are considering going into a partnership now or in the future, you'll want to make sure that you do everything you can to help that partnership succeed. To that end, Business Partnership Essentials contains valuable (even invaluable) information. It walks you through every phase of the process—from deciding if you truly want to partner with the person you are considering, to planning, building and running your business on a daily basis and beyond—all the way to a planned exit strategy (a critical yet often overlooked consideration). If you already have a partner, this book will serve to enrich your partnership and give you renewed confidence in knowing that you're taking the necessary steps to ensure that your partnership (and, therefore, your business) runs as smoothly as a well-oiled machine.

How I Came to Write this Book

In order to understand what you will learn from this book, it is helpful to understand the motivations and experiences that led to this book. I've acquired my knowledge about business partnerships in a number of ways and over many years. Those experiences became pieces in a fascinating master puzzle that ultimately inspired me to focus all of my accumulated expertise on business partnership coaching. My long-term mission has been to use my hard-won knowledge to increase the success rates of business partners, co-founders and joint ventures.

As a child and through my teen years, I observed a number of partnerships in my extended family. Among my family and friends, these business partnerships included a dry cleaning establishment, air conditioning and heating company, plumbing supply business and a chain of DIY home center stores. Three of these partnerships succeeded; the fourth did not. Family meetings were held in my grandmother's kitchen to resolve some of the issues involving tension between close relatives who were in business together. Looking back, those meetings and subsequent conversations helped me to understand the role of personal relationships in these businesses. I saw first-hand that the partners needed to communicate with each other about their work. I couldn't help but notice how important transparency, trust and respect were in these relationships. Those who talked to each other and worked out their differences and difficulties one step at a time were more successful.

I observed the effects of actions that may have been well intentioned, but basically amounted to family interference. Taking on a partner, because the family expected it, didn't work. In the case of my family, that fourth partnership failed due to a mismatch and lack of synergy between the parties involved. It was uncomfortable and tense from the get-go. One person had been a successful business owner for a few years, and the other was a hard-working, blue-collar factory employee with no entrepreneurial experience. While it began with the best of intentions and high hopes for success, the forced partnership between these two family members ultimately crashed and burned.

Thereafter, I was privy to the ins-and-outs of a successful business partnership when my husband chose the right partner and built a chain of home center stores. After a good run and a change in their individual visions, the partnership dissolved amicably using the buy-sell exit strategy that we will discuss later in the book.

The next puzzle pieces about business partnerships fell into place through my work in attaining a master's degree and PhD in social work, coupled with an LCSW California State license allow me to practice psychotherapy, which I did for a number of years. The skills and knowledge that I acquired on that career path informs my business partnership coaching and helps my clients have healthy, more functional relationships. My therapy and social work background have given me the knowledge and people skills that I use in coaching those in business. I am equipped to deal with the matrix of relationships within a business, but I don't give expert advice in legal issues, finance, business technology and other areas that require a different expertise. I recommend that my clients seek out the best in these fields.

My experience as a coach for the past few decades has added even more puzzle pieces to complete the overall picture of business partnerships. I began as a career coach, focusing primarily on lawyers who wanted to transition to another career, often ones that more fully expressed their inner selves—their hopes, dreams, ambitions and secret desires. Over the years, other clients who were seeking a career change from other professions began to show up. Among them were clients who dreamed of being entrepreneurs. Some were already in partnerships or at least considering them. As I began to work with these individuals, I became aware of the high failure rate of business partnerships. This confirmed what I'd learned years earlier.

As a coach, I help partners build, maintain or repair their relationships. The businesses, not the partners themselves, are my clients, and because of this, together we examine the power that the individuals' relationship has on their day-to-day operations and the bottom line. Unlike my focus as a therapist, where the goal was to heal and repair old patterns, the goal in business partnership coaching is to circumvent those old patterns and build higher functioning ones from this point forward.

Tip: The quality of the relationship between the partners is the key to their business success.

The old straw "a jack of all trades is a master of none" is true; that's why it's an old straw. I am a strong advocate of the idea that everyone ought to seek their niche and do what they love. I take my own advice. I love working with partners to change the dismal landscape of failure to one of wild, bright success. I've been doing this for about 20 years now, and I've been taking copious notes. *Business*

Partnership Essentials is the result of this experience and note taking. My hope is that anyone who is considering walking away from a partnership out of frustration, anger, despair or fear of failure will instead pick up this book, follow its instructions and allow it to inspire conversations, share experiences and strengthen the determination to succeed.

How to Use This Book

The book is divided into five parts.

Part I pertains to choosing the right partner, as doing this correctly is crucial to your success. The relationship between the partner owners or business co-founders sets the tone for everyone involved and directly affects the bottom line. If you are already in a partnership and have overlooked some essentials at the outset, now would be the time to put them in place.

Part II will guide you through what is needed to set a strong foundation, including the completion of written documents that clarify and solidify every aspect of your relationship from start through exit strategy. I will also address how to prepare for the unexpected.

Part III will discuss how to find your daily rhythm through productive ongoing communication with your partners, managers and teams; this will ensure that your partnership continues to thrive for years to come.

Part IV takes a slight departure from the rest of the book to address separate (yet related) information about joint ventures and a growing trend towards business collaboration in general, especially businesses that support causes.

Part V consists of two appendices that you will find well worth the time to read. Appendix A, *Keys to Effectively Delegating and Having Time for Yourself* is brief, but its lessons can be life-changing. Appendix B, *Business Partnership Success Meter* is a two page test of how likely your partnership is to succeed. It can be taken at any time. It is best not to look at page two until you have completed the questions on page one.

I've included many real-life stories in this book as case studies to illustrate what makes for a successful partnership. These stories fall into two categories:1) successful partners who I interviewed and who gave me permission to share their experiences, including some of my clients; and 2) scenarios that are real, but in which the names and identifying information have been changed to protect privacy. I've also woven in a handful of partnerships that are well known, even legendary. I've chosen not just successes but a number of "failure" stories because of the value they offer in learning. Some of the case studies may sound somewhat repetitious. This is intentional on my part to drive home important points about basic principles and problems that are typical in all partnership successes and failures. Pay attention to the common themes in these stories.

To glean the most benefit from these vignettes, read them reflectively, as if they are your story. See yourself as one and then the other partner. Put yourself into the shoes of each and experience the respective joys, pains, fears, desires and personalities. Ask yourself if you would have reacted similarly or differently than your partner(s). Can you see how willingness to understand the other partner might have led to a different outcome? Or in the case of the successful partnerships, if one or the other had instead displayed unwillingness to move, trust, be honest or compromise, how would it have reversed the direction away from success?

You will find essential questions, such as the ones above, as well as tips, interspersed throughout the narrative. Use these to reflect a little further and deeper on your current or future partnership situation.

Yet bear in mind that *Business Partnership Essentials* is not just a one-time-use reference. Change is a constant in life, and the growth of a business is no exception. For this reason, I advise that you revisit the book for periodic check-ups to determine if you are still on track, as well as where you can or need to improve. Doing so will provide a big payoff. In fact, keep *Business Partnership Essentials* on hand through all the phases of your business—from start-up through years to come—as a practical and effective guide to your success.

It is my hope that both you and your partner(s) will utilize this book's guidelines, both individually and together, in order to successfully navigate your business journey from beginning to fruition. Throughout these pages, any references to "you" apply equally to your partner(s). Congratulations on taking this important first step for your future business success. By strengthening your business partnership bond and building a successful enterprise, you will be doing nothing short of helping to change the global economy.

Additional Materials in Support of the Book

In addition to the text, there are four quite effective, tested, supplementary items available that complement the book and that you will want to download. These items are all available on the Products page at bizpartnerpro.com.

Free Mini-book

The Guide for Choosing the Right Business Partner: We are pleased to announce that this mini-book is no longer for sale and is available as a **free download** on the Product page at bizpartnerpro.com.

This 12-page guide walks you through the conversations you will need to have before you or a potential business partner, co-founder, or joint venture partner take the next step. The process of doing this will go a long way toward solidifying the right partnership and prepare you for the next step: completing the *Business Partnership Agreement Template.*

Purchase the Indispensable BPAT

Business Partnership Agreement Template: This clear, concise, easy-to-follow 33-page guide is where you and your partner will record the decisions you have made that define your partnership relationship and the way your business functions. Through years of experience, I have refined this document to maximize its effectiveness as the most important step in creating a lasting partnership. This template and the What If Scenario Handbook to Prepare for the Unexpected Before it Occurs, are the keystones to documenting the mutual agreements which will provide for a successful partnership. Find it here: www.bizpartnerpro.com/bpat.

Now *Free* with the Purchase of Business Partnership Agreement Template

What If Scenario Handbook to Prepare for the Unexpected Before it Occurs: This 56-page e-book, formerly $49.99, is now free with the purchase of the *Business Partnership Agreement Template*, and is the perfect complement to it, laying the groundwork for dealing with potential problems and sensitive issues in advance. It walks you through conversations and the decision-making process for crises that may occur. Not all of them will occur, of course, and the list of potential problems is not all-inclusive, but this book covers the most likely scenarios. This product is no longer available separately. For more details, see the Products page on bizpartnerpro.com.

Purchase the Joint Ventures Agreement Template

Joint Ventures Agreement Template: Similar to the *Business Partnership Agreement Template*, this 34-page guide is geared toward two businesses doing a limited joint venture rather than establishing a new business together. Following the instructions on this template will help to solidify the relationship between joint venture partners and avoid pitfalls that can lead to failure. This template can be used over again for any number of JVs. Find it at bizpartnerpro.com/jvtemplate.

How You Can Work with Dr. Lehavi

For information about coaching with Dr. Dorene Lehavi visit this page:
http://www.bizpartnerpro.com/contact-bizpartner-pro/.
For more information, email info@bizpartnerpro.com.

Dorene Lehavi, PhD

Part I: **Choosing the Right Partner**

Chapter 1
Hook Up or Stay Solo: The Benefits of a Partnership

"Is doing business with a partner better than going at it alone? My answer is yes.
Nothing in business is more rewarding.
Working together is much better than working alone."

—Michael Eisner, CEO, Walt Disney Co.

Business is 20% technology and 80% psychology. This sentiment was shared with me a few years ago when I visited with Dr. William Crookston, now a retired professor of Clinical Entrepreneurship at the Lloyd Greif Center for Entrepreneurial Studies at the University of Southern California's Marshall Business School. Dr. Crookston admitted that business schools teach the 20% but give little attention to the other 80%.

My career, and this book, focus on the 80% psychology—or, as I prefer to say, the "relationships of business." Whenever and wherever you learned about business, chances are you were taught that it is supposed to be objective and devoid of emotion. What I know for sure contradicts this mindset. The truth is, the avoidance of feelings is impossible. After all, we're only human. As a business person, you may have developed a habit of denying your emotions, or not acknowledging and dealing with them, but they exist and are influencing you whether you recognize it or not. I challenge you to relate to business terms like "success," "failure," "money," "cash flow," "teamwork," "production," "management," "hire," "delegate" and others without having them bring up a tinge of emotion. Perhaps you feel happy, fearful, anxious, proud or shameful. You have your own distinct personality, which you don't leave outside the office door. Maybe you are ambitious, joyful or dedicated. Perhaps you are prone to procrastination or you're a workaholic. What ruffles your feathers a little? What pushes your buttons and sends you into an emotional meltdown? Maybe you love the people you work with or are constantly annoyed by one or more. Are you competitive or a team player? Well, you are feeling whatever it is that you're feeling because business correlates to your very humanity. Although you may believe that you can take one part of you to work and keep the other part separate for your personal life, it is not possible. Pushing down your feelings or pretending they're not real is an inefficient and unhealthy way to live. Your work affects all areas of your life because it is a large part of your identity and a source of relationships that fill your life. For better or worse, it is an outgrowth of who you are at any given moment

DOI 10.1515/9781547400188-001

in time, carrying with it all that came before in your life that brought you to "now" and prepared you (or not) to do whatever you are doing.

As I will repeatedly point out (because it is so key), all business is about relationships, a place where feelings thrive. The relationship between the partners sets the tone for all involved—from employees, customers and family members to the community and much more. When a local business closes, the loss is felt far beyond the personal lives of the partners; it extends into the community itself.

Because of the fallout—emotional and otherwise—that occurs when business partnerships fail, it behooves all entrepreneurs, solos, co-founders, partners and joint ventures to recognize the ripple effect that results from the way they conduct their businesses. Putting personal gain aside in favor of what must be done, without counting hours and minutes of who is doing more, will go a long way in making the partnership and business work well. The goal should be to have a well-run, profitable business, and the partners are there to make that happen. As we will explore, the attributes of trust, mutual respect and ongoing communication are essential keys. To this end, try the following exercise:

Around the Table Picture a conference table where two new partners are sitting on opposite sides discussing their roles in the business. They are making important decisions about the operations of the business, and about how expenses and profits will be divided. The discussion is about "the individuals." Each one is thinking about what they are putting in and getting back. Now try this: Change the seating arrangement so that the partners are sitting next to each other, and "the business" is opposite them.

From this vantage point, they can look at the business's needs in order to fulfill the vision they have of it. The discussion and decision making should focus on meeting operational needs such as finance, technology, production, sales and marketing. They decide who will be responsible for each. This sitting arrangement is more conducive to what is needed to succeed than the first scenario.

Advantages of a Partnership

Many solo owners of businesses occasionally toy with the idea of having a partner, yet remain ambivalent. In order to find the right partner, there has to be determination coupled with a clear picture of why you want a partner, as well as what each of you should bring to the table. That's just the tip of the iceberg. There is much more, but let's start by looking at the many advantages of joining forces versus going solo.

The End of Isolation

As those who are sole proprietors know well, it can be lonely at the top. As a solo entrepreneur, you are more likely to be doing most or all the work in your business yourself, rather than having time to build and expand it. You are most often alone in the decision-making process, as well as strategizing and visioning. With a partner, you will have someone with whom to share and discuss ideas, and weather the highs and lows. As a partner, you will also increase your opportunities to find time to build and grow the business as you share the day-to-day responsibilities.

Shared Risks and Responsibilities

Partnerships make the distribution of responsibilities possible. The fear and anxiety associated with taking risks can be mitigated with someone at your side who can offer reassurance and support. A partner may provide needed capital or a robust client base. He or she will see things from a different angle, thus expanding the company's vision. Partnerships offer a chance to delegate some of the responsibility to another who is equally committed to the success of the company.

Aligned Individual Strengths

Sole proprietors are left to do most of the work on their own, regardless of personal strengths and weaknesses. As partners, the work can be more closely aligned with each person's strengths, thus allowing everyone to focus on the work that best suits them. *Inc. Magazine* has dubbed Michael E. Gerber "the World's #1 Small Business Guru." In Gerber's book, *The E-Myth: Why Most Small Businesses Don't Work and What to Do About It* (and subsequent *E-Myth* books) he says, "one plus one should equal three." With each individual bringing his or her unique strengths to the table, new possibilities become feasible and, indeed, one plus one begins to equal three.

Two Heads (and Hearts) are Better Than One

The relationship between partners should be sufficiently intimate to allow each to be vulnerable with the other, without fear of being poorly judged for weaknesses, fears or discomfort of any kind. In strong, healthy partnerships, the partners are trustworthy people and will comfortably challenge each other, allowing for an examination of the issues from multiple perspectives. This can result in a higher volume of creative ideas and a larger offering of products and client services because more minds, hearts and souls are working towards a common goal. Conversely, spending time brainstorming with a partner can stop a solo decision maker from making a costly mistake.

Why Do You Want a Business Partner, Honestly?

Before you decide to bring on a business partner, it's important to consider why you want one in the first place. Some reasons are better than others. The important point is to be honest with yourself first, then be willing to be openly candid with the partner you are considering.

In my experience, all successful partnerships say that trust is the most important element in the relationship. As author Stephen M. R. Covey asserts in his 2006 bestselling book, *The Speed of Trust*, "The ability to establish, extend, and restore trust with all stakeholders–customers, business partners, investors and coworkers–is the key leadership competency of the new, global economy." He further explains that today's leaders are rediscovering trust as they see it with new eyes. Looking beyond the common view of trust as a soft, social virtue, they're learning to see it as a critical, highly relevant performance multiplier.

Trust is built on openness, transparency, commitment to each other as well as the business, and is the basis for building it. So, begin with being open and honest with what you are thinking. Tell your prospective partner that you want them because of their financial wherewithal, their reputation, customer base, connections or skill sets. Perhaps you simply don't want all the responsibility on your shoulders alone. Can you tell them what you bring to the table even if you believe it is of lesser value for whatever reason?

This kind of openness will endear the right partner to you. After acknowledging whatever it is you can, then discuss important details for correcting any concerns about the situation, including a fair differential in financial compensation or time off. Perhaps the differential would be limited in time and evened out as certain benchmarks are met. All kinds of arrangements can be discussed and adopted when there is trust and respect based on transparent communication. By contrast, be aware that secrets and hidden agendas can create bad blood in a partnership relationship, dooming it from the start.

A Final Word About Going Solo

So yes, there are great benefits to having a partner, but partnerships are not for everyone. It is unwise to enter into a partnership if it's not right for you or if the person you are considering is not a good fit. Always trust your instincts, pay attention to red flags, and if things don't feel right, shake hands and walk away. A bad partnership can be worse than a bad marriage, and partnership divorces can be even more complex, costly and ugly than any divorce from marriage. As mostly anyone who has been through such a traumatic breakup can attest, it's better to go it alone than spend years unwinding from physical, emotional and financial misery with the wrong person.

TIP: It's better to remain solo than to choose the wrong partner(s).

***

So how do you even begin looking for your partnership match? When clients ask me how they can best find a partner, I advise them to tell everyone they know that they are looking, to attend meetings in their field, and to connect with networking groups and associations belonging to their industry. I also advise them to check online and join global groups such as CoFoundersLab.com, which offers a free membership and helps members find their business match. It is encouraging that Shahab Kaviani, co-founder of CoFoundersLab (a Onevest Company), notes "a growing trend by founders to be more selective in choosing the right partner."

Before reaching out and beginning these networking activities, make doubly sure that you are very clear about your motivations for wanting a partner, what you are offering as a partner and what you are seeking. As a start, ask yourself a few of these basic yet essential questions and take some time to ponder the answers beyond the first ones that pop into your mind.

ESSENTIAL QUESTIONS:

— Why do you want a partner?
— Why would you be a good partner?

—   What do you bring to the table?
—   How do you rate yourself as a communicator?
—   How do you rate yourself as a team player?

Let's move on now to the three main components to building a successful partnership. They are simple to understand, challenging to do, but well worth it.

Chapter 2
Your Significant "Business Other": Choosing the Right Partner

"If you fail to get it right at the start, it may cost you dearly to fix it later."

–Curtis E. Sahakian, author,
Corporate Partnering: A How-To Handbook

The above quote is rather harsh, so I hesitated to open the chapter with it but forged ahead because what Sahakian says is true. This step is where it all begins and ends. If you get this right, then no matter what business you are in, your partnership will stand a decent chance of being successful. And so, we begin with the first of three crucial components in building a successful partnership: Choosing the right partner. This step is of paramount importance, yet it is where many people make a monumental mistake. Don't be intimidated by Sahakian's hard-won wisdom. As I walk you through this first phase of the process, you will discover that finding the right person is not only doable, it can prove to be a deeply and thoroughly satisfying experience.

As I've mentioned, many business partners would attest that their relationship is analogous to a marriage—and for good reason. Our cultural fascination with relationships often focuses on romantic partnerships rather than business connections, but as I say in the Introduction, marriage and business are more alike than you may realize. Both involve people working together to create and maintain a strong, successful, abundant, long-term, trusting relationship. They are required to bring unwavering commitment, a willingness to be transparent, always improving communication skills, and a shared vision for where each partner would like the relationship to go. The principles of giving, communicating, paying attention on a regular basis, trusting, and showing regard for each other are basic attributes that are critical to success in both marriage and business partnerships.

Before I have you saying "I do," however, I'd like to engage you in a little bit of pre-marital counseling, if you will, to save you from making critical mistakes in your business partnership relationship. Let me share two stories about partners who chose well and created successful alliances.

DOI 10.1515/9781547400188-002

Compromise Improves the Bottom Line

Molly and Sam opened an Asian fusion restaurant in the outskirts of Montreal, Canada. In the beginning, Sam took control of making the important decisions and kept Molly, whose personality is non-assertive and non-confrontational, in the background. Molly had been complying with his demands, but eventually a lack of communication and not behaving like true partners became a liability.

One day when Sam was not there, Molly made some decisions about the menu that enraged Sam when he returned. Tension grew and customers, wait staff and employees in the kitchen felt it. The atmosphere was not the relaxing environment that people desired in their dining experience and business began to fall off. At that point, a friend suggested that they contact me. Many partners in this situation would allow the situation to deteriorate and would ultimately join the 70% of failed partnerships.

Sam and Molly were committed to the restaurant and to their relationship, as troubled as it was. They were both open to taking an honest look at their own responsibility and behavior that got them to this danger point, and they called me for a rescue. With practice, Molly learned to openly express her hurt feelings of being treated with disrespect and not as an equal partner by Sam. It was equally difficult for Sam to relinquish his ground as "boss and decision maker." Their respective behavior had been disrespectful, contentious and dysfunctional. After six months of coaching, their working relationship had completely changed. Their newfound respect for each other helped to recreate the pleasant dining environment that their customers and employees wanted. As a result, their business flourished.

ESSENTIAL QUESTIONS: *Had Molly and Sam spent enough time getting to know each other for the purpose of choosing the right partner, do you think they would have gone into a partnership in the first place? What and when would you have done differently as Molly? Sam?*

The following case study illustrates the value of having good communication from the start of the partnership.

Even Near Perfect Partnerships Benefit from Good Communication

John Barrentine and Chuck Marquardt of Red Real Estate Group in Los Angeles, California (redrealestategroup.com) have what could be the poster-perfect partnership—both in their personal lives as a married couple, as well as in business. Wisely, they have set boundaries between the two. They trust each other's judgment completely and there are no battles. If one feels very strongly about something, his view is accepted. Generally, if there is a disagreement, they discuss it until they arrive at a decision that works for both, never using the words "right" or "wrong."

John answered "yes" when I asked if there is at least one problem between them. He is sometimes uncomfortable with Chuck's communication style with clients. He told me about it in good humor; however, John, who is more genteel and soft-spoken, affirmed that despite his discomfort with Chuck's more direct style, he is willing to overlook it because the outcome is always good and in line with their shared values and goals. Because of that and the importance of their relationship both in business and outside of it, he is willing to make this compromise to his comfort zone. Because they talk about everything, Chuck is aware and sensitive to John's feelings.

ESSENTIAL QUESTIONS: *If something your partner did made you uncomfortable, would you bring it up or avoid addressing it? John made the compromise but only after talking about it, so Chuck knows exactly how he feels. Do you think Chuck should change his behavior out of respect for John's discomfort or is it better that John just accepts it?*

Keep in mind what you've just learned from these two stories as I throw into the mix a few about other partnerships that didn't fare so well. The most common scenario that I encounter in my coaching work is two or more individuals who have the same idea for a business and are excited about joining forces. These individuals may have complementary skills, which can give them even more reason to move ahead with their idea. They rush ahead, fueled by their excitement, without taking the time to get to know one another well enough.

Before long, these individuals have acquired the necessary financing and have gone into business together. Soon after or down the road, problems arise as the broader, deeper issues of personality, personal goals, varying work styles, different visions and values, and issues such as risk tolerance and the demands of family life begin to surface. Many of these misunderstandings are due to a lack of initial discussions and could have been addressed and even circumvented. Left unspoken and unresolved, troubles begin to snowball. The potential for a full-blown avalanche has already begun to form.

The following story is an example of what can happen when people rush into a partnership before first sufficiently getting to know each other.

Doomed from the Start

When I met Theodore and Sandra via Skype they were too angry with each other even to be in the same room, and Theodore stood his ground in his unwillingness to work toward a solution. Theodore was a talented hair stylist with a reputation for being good at his job. Sandra was on the business side, managing a different salon. They met at a birthday party of a mutual friend and began talking about their respective dreams of opening their own salon. Theodore and Sandra spent little time getting to know each other. Following the party, they enthusiastically decided to move ahead with their business plan. They based their decision almost entirely on their complementary skills and desire to have their own salon. With the support of each of their spouses, they mortgaged their homes and bought a site in an affluent area of Chicago. Many of their loyal clients followed them, and with their convenient location and smart advertising, they quickly attracted a large number of new clients.

Within less than two years of opening their business, they broke even and were beginning to see some significant income. After another year, however, Theodore's resentment festered and exploded. Sandra was a mother and she frequently had to leave the salon to pick up her children and do other motherly duties, such as occasionally stay at home with her sick child or take a turn volunteering at their school. She was conscientious about the business and always made sure that all back office duties and operations were well executed. Theodore acknowledged that fact. But he began to feel that he was more valuable to the success of the business than Sandra because of the experience and talent he brought to the floor—experience and talent that she did not possess. He thought of himself as a "rock star" hair stylist and his feelings led him to become verbally abusive to Sandra. Soon employees and clients began to notice the tension.

Theodore would gladly have bought the business from Sandra, but he didn't have the financial means. Both were tied to the misery of their daily routine at the salon because of their respective mortgage and family obligations. Although Sandra was open to discussing how they could make things better, Theodore was unwilling to engage in any talks about repairing the problem. Out of respect for the friend who referred them to me, he did agree for the three of us to meet. At our meeting, he stated his position but would not engage in any conversation about a compromise or repair. He avoided even speaking directly to Sandra. Because of his unwillingness, the situation was sadly beyond help. He had not only decided that his "celebrity" status was the reason for their success, but also had built such a deep resentment toward Sandra that he couldn't stand to be near her. He remained adamant in his insistence that their partnership relationship was over.

I subsequently learned that they struggled together for another year and found a way to close the business. This was a costly event that affected not just the partners but their families, employees, vendors, customers, landlord and the neighborhood where they were considered a valued asset.

It is sad to see a situation in which two opportunities were ignored that could have led to Sandra and Theodore's situation turning out differently. The first is: if after the birthday party they had engaged in the discussions I describe in this book, they may not have gone into a partnership at all. The second is: had they come for coaching much earlier before overwhelmingly negative emotions ruled, we could have either repaired the partnership or at least planned for a more friendly and respectful exit.

As in any relationship, partners must be prepared to roll up their sleeves and work through their issues. If partners are unable or unwilling to face their challenges, their partnerships will be in jeopardy. Both divorce and broken business partnerships can range anywhere on the continuum from amicable to tragically destructive. When partnerships dissolve, other people often take sides and vilify one of the partners. Partners on the brink of breaking up cause great strife in their personal lives and the people surrounding them, as often happens in a divorce when extended families and friends become involved.

ESSENTIAL QUESTION: *This partnership skipped the most important step, in choosing the right partner. They probably would not have gone into business with each other had they done it. Once in business, it is essential that every partnership begin and remain open, honest, transparent and communicate regularly...at least weekly...addressing what will become a source of growing tension if they don't. Even better is to approach your partner at the beginning of a contentious feeling and make a point to address it before it becomes explosive or so embedded that it's impossible to talk about it. "What would you have done?"*

***

Trust, respect and likability are vitally important to your partnership. These traits should evolve as you get to know each other. All of that got lost between Theodore and Sandra. Beware of signing on the dotted line and committing to a partnership until you have reached a level of mutual respect, trust and friendship. If you do not like or respect your partner and if those qualities aren't growing as you spend more time together, listen to that ever-present voice inside you that says, according to spiritual guide and teacher Lester Levenson, "what you know before you start to think." Walk away if that voice is warning you that this person is not likable, not trustworthy, not respectful, non-communicative or in any other way the wrong person for you.

TIP: Be aware of the possibility that your desire for the partnership to work might be pushing you to overlook warning signs.

Three Essential Words: Communication, Transparency and Responsibility

How do you avert landing in a partnership situation like Sandra and Theodore, and instead find a match like John and Chuck? The three most important characteristics to ensure a successful business partnership relationship are communication, transparency and responsibility. Each of you must be willing to be as open as you would be with your spouse. Yes, that means you must be able to communicate honestly about everything. Additionally, all partners must take 100% responsibility to ensure that everything the business needs is provided.

When communication is clear, you've taken the most important step to preserving your business partnership and all of your relationships. However, even with clear communication, it is reasonable to expect that even the best partnerships will at some point face a communication breakdown. The smart thing to do is to keep the dialogue open and friendly so objections can be discussed as they occur. This way, everyone wins and the business stays solvent. Simply stated, the key to successful outcomes is communication!

When people become hostile, overpowering, antagonistic, non-communicative, disagreeable and confrontational, everybody loses. How miserable it must be to go to work every day in such an atmosphere! The health of a relationship is always based on communication, and the main tool of good communication is listening with the intent to hear, understand and even to try to see another person's viewpoint. It does not mean giving up your stand, although you may. Part of it is being willing to change your perspective after truly listening. Likewise, it also means that you will have the opportunity to be heard and possibly change someone else's mind. We will talk about good communication and listening skills in Chapter 12.

In my coaching practice, I see people (some quite hateful, unfortunately) who are afraid to listen because they strongly oppose and even fear others' viewpoints. Fear, anger and hatred are no basis for getting anything good accomplished. That sentence bears repeating: Fear, anger and hatred lead to nothing productive. I've noticed over the years that most failures can be traced to a deteriorated relationship that started to tank when misunderstandings arose and there wasn't a willingness to respectfully listen and disagree, if necessary. That is initially what happened in the following scenario but, fortunately, the partners were able to turn things around.

TIP: Commit to open and honest communication. This is the only sure way to maintain and grow your relationship.

Everyone Loses When Playing the Blame Game

An insurance agency run by Tom, Peter and three management level employees (who were made to feel that they were also part of the partnership, although they weren't officially) called me in crisis mode when they lost their biggest client. No one saw it coming and, until then, they were all under the impression that the business team respected and supported each other and the company was successful. With the sudden loss of this client, each began accusing the other of not doing their jobs and being responsible for the loss. I spent a day with them, first speaking privately with each one. Learning that they could trust me to keep their confidences, the three managers each revealed how they felt their opinions were not valued by the owners and other team members and, in fact, were never even solicited. They each harbored resentment and anger. Janet was the only female, which added another level of feeling discounted by the others.

In a group meeting that afternoon, each of them trusted that I would not break their confidences but would be the supporter to help them express their feelings. As a result, each one took their turn sharing how discounted and hurt they felt. Tom and Peter were shocked to hear this and seemed very sincere in their apologies and promises to correct the situation. I helped them commit to meeting schedules with agendas, and most importantly to actually listen with open minds to each other. Everyone participated in more clearly defining their respective responsibilities. Their willingness to be responsive created a totally different work environment, which ultimately improved the atmosphere in the office and, of course, the bottom line.

ESSENTIAL QUESTIONS: *What false assumptions had been made by the CEOs prior to this crisis? What would you have done to avoid this happening? Do you think each of the people on this team will change their mode of communication going forward?*

The following case study speaks to the importance of the third key word in any partnership arrangement, "responsibility." As I mention above, all partners must be willing to take full responsibility for providing whatever the business needs at any given time. This is actually one of the inherent benefits of forming a partnership. Often sole proprietors are required to put their businesses on hold when personal issues arise—a death in the family, illness or accident, a wedding or graduation. These events can wind up requiring time and attention that pulls business owners away from work. With a partner, that person can keep the business going while the other partner attends to personal matters.

I've Got Your Back

Dale Bell and Harry Wiland have been friends for more than 40 years, and they happen to be the award winning co-CEOs of the Media Policy Center in Santa Monica, California (mediapolicycenter.org), a company that makes documentaries about social value. During our in-person interview, Dale and Harry spoke about what has made their 15-year business partnership so strong. What impressed me the most is that they always have each other's back, and never notice who is working more or less at any given time. They clearly have a deep regard for each other, including the demands of their respective lives outside of business. Without a second thought, each jumps in when the other needs a backup.

It's vital in a good partnership always to focus on the big picture and be committed to doing what is needed, even if it's going the extra mile when your partner can't. An attitude toward your partner that reinforces the "I've got your back" sentiment is a strong indicator of a solid relationship. The right chemistry and determination from the beginning can eventually transform into a solid support system for each other, in good times and in bad.

ESSENTIAL QUESTIONS: *How would you feel if your partner was continuously able to finish work in less time than you finished yours? Would you be able to communicate your feelings about it? If you were the partner who finished in less time and heard this concern, what would be your response?*

Improved Communication Benefits All Your Relationships

One of the many benefits of improving your communication, transparency and sense of responsibility within your business partnership is that these qualities can carry over into your personal life, as well. That's what happened to Tony, who, following a coaching session that rescued his partnership, told me that the communication skills he learned from our working together not only mended his relationship with his partner, Larry, but also showed him how poorly he had been treating people in his personal life. It's not that Tony is a bad guy. He simply came into his relationships with the attitude that it was always about him and what he was getting from the other person. Unfortunately, this is not an uncommon approach in relationships. In business, Tony lorded over Larry because he believed he was the more competent one and, in fact, had the most equity in the business. Larry, in turn, was happy to avoid meeting with him.

When they both finally noticed that the business was in a downward spiral, they were forced to talk. Finger pointing and screaming that went nowhere led them to call me for help. With me guiding the conversations, the volume was turned down and problems were addressed. Tony became painfully aware that his attitude of "knowing best" and talking down to Larry was a major part of the problem. To his credit, Tony was able to see how he did this in his personal relationships, as well. (Generally speaking, how we do one thing is how we do mostly everything!) Now he is committed to changing his behavior both in business and in his personal life.

Communication in the Online World

The Internet and social media have led to more opportunities to build relationships with potential clients and others and, at the same time, more opportunities for miscommunication. In today's multi-media environment where emails and texting are relied upon heavily to communicate, it is not surprising that messages can be misconstrued. Have you ever misinterpreted someone's meaning in an email, text or chat message, or did they misunderstand you? Did that lead to clarification or even an apology? It's important to be that open and vulnerable. Are you?

Your online presence—whether it's your website, emails, blog posts, comments on social media sites, or anything else—is "communicating" on your behalf, as well. What does your website convey, not just about your business, but about you as the owners? The same with your Facebook, Twitter, Instagram, blog and other social profiles: What impression is the outside world getting of you from these news feeds and sites?

The point is that it all falls under the umbrella of "relationship." Just because you are communicating virtually doesn't mean that your message is being received as you intend. For example, some of us will not engage with a business that does not disclose who the owners are on the company's website, and even what they look like. I appreciate a friendly photo so I can "connect" with the owners. There is much more that can be said about the subject of "online reputation" and how it helps you relate to others (and them to you), but that would be another book. I would just like to remind you that clear communication, trust and openness are as important in the cyber world as they are in person.

***

Making a commitment to solid communication, transparency and responsibility is important not just in the initial stages of choosing the right partner, but ongoing as you get to know each other and determine if you truly are a right fit. Next, I will guide you through what I call the "dating" period of your new partnership. As always, patience and open-mindedness are necessary to determine whether your new "match" is actually a good one.

Chapter 3
Getting to Know You:
Playing the Field with a Purpose

"It's extremely important that you let people know where you stand–what motivates you, how you operate, what your expectations are, etcetera."

–Doug Conant,
CEO of Campbell Soup Company

By now, you've been doing your due diligence by defining what you require in a business partner and what assets you bring to the bargaining table. At the same time, you've been scoping out prospective partners and what they might each add to the equation. You may even believe that you've found the right one.

This is a critical time to keep in mind that there's no good reason to rush to the business partnership altar. Continue getting to know one another even better so that you will be as sure as possible that you are right for each other. If you are already in a partnership, use the same guidelines that I outline in this chapter to clarify areas that you might have overlooked or misunderstood in the early days of your partnership. Elicit help from a business coach if you can't have these discussions without someone to facilitate. (I strongly recommend, by the way, that you avoid using a friend or relative to do this. You will need someone who is completely impartial.)

BONUS: *In Appendix B, you will find a quick and easy Business Partnership Success Meter to assess how your existing partnership rates and where you need to improve. If you are not yet in a partnership, look it over now anyway, because it will show you the elements that you will want in your successful partnership. Use it again over time to measure your improvement.*

How to Date Your Potential Partner

The most effective way to choose a business partner is similar to the best way to choose a spouse. Chances are that you will spend more time with your business partner than you do with your spouse, so taking the time to make a smart choice is crucial. Court each other in an effort to become more familiar with each other's personality, preferences, values, work styles and habits, just like you would a potential husband or wife.

DOI 10.1515/9781547400188-003

The dating period is when and where you will make some of your foundational decisions. Writing down your goals and objectives for yourself and the partnership can help immensely. If you don't like to write, use a digital voice recorder or some other device that you can refer to again. Try the exercise below to expand on the questions you began to ask yourself in the previous section.

Starting with your own goals and objectives, answer the following questions. Then look at them again and go deeper. Be honest about why you would be a good partner; or, if you have a partner, answer them according to your present situation. Share these questions with your partner(s) and ask them to do the same.

- Why do/did I want a partner or co-founder?
- What kind of partner or co-founder am I or would I be?
- How flexible am I willing to be?
- What vision do I have for what this partnership should look like?
- What am I looking for (did I look for) in a partner or co-founder?
- What strengths do I bring to the collaboration?
- What are my weaknesses?
- What about me might annoy my partner?

Once you have done this exercise, read it over or listen to it carefully, give it to your potential partner and read or listen to theirs. Sit down and discuss your thoughts, feelings and insights about each other's answers. Are you on the same page with your potential or established partner(s) beyond your desire for the same business and believing that you have complementary skills? Where are you not aligned and how can you start to make some improvements? How did you score on the Business Partnership Success Meter (mentioned above)?

ESSENTIAL QUESTIONS: *Use the above questions to review information about your previous business partnerships, as well. How would you have answered them differently knowing what you know now? Would it have changed the outcome of your partnership? What changes have occurred in you? What did you learn about yourself and about partnerships in general?*

Continue Being Open and Honest During the Dating Process

I've already touched upon the significance of transparency and trust. Let's stay with this topic a bit longer, as it is imperative for partnership success. In close relationships, transparency should be the rule. If you and your business partner cannot share everything about yourselves, how you feel about things, and be able to talk about them, then your partnership can easily get into trouble. Remember that, with business partners, it's the same rule that applies for married couples: if they don't talk about everything, share feelings and resolve issues, they run into problems. Hiding, avoiding, secretly resenting, harboring dissatisfaction are all words and phrases that have no place in successful marriages or business partnerships. Openness coupled with a commitment to rectify any problems will ensure the ultimate goal of a long life of happiness and business success. What happened between the two partners in the following story makes this point quite clearly.

Avoiding Confrontation Leads to Confrontation

I was introduced to Jean, the owner of a well-respected mortgage company in Dallas, Texas, when I attended a conference there. She is very well known in her local business community and told me that she and her partner have a great relationship. (This is often the response that I get when I tell people what I do.) I was told that Jean is a great networker who frequents every event around town that she can. I couldn't help but notice that when telling me about the great relationship she has with her partner, she added, "I don't think he resents me being out so much." That comment told me two things: 1) she and her partner don't really communicate because she doesn't really know how he feels, and 2) he likely does resent it, or else she wouldn't have used that word. She might have a hunch that he does, but prefers not to address it. Like Jean, he may also prefer to not discuss it, so they both play the game that all is well.

This problem (as I would call it) cannot be resolved on its own. If there ever was reasonably good communication between them, it was now being lost in the avoidance of each other in order to protect themselves from the truth: that all is not so well. It is easy to go on, day-in and day-out avoiding communication. The solution is for partners to have regularly scheduled meetings at least weekly where all issues are put on the table discussed and resolved. Avoiding talking about most anything related to the relationship and the business is a sure prescription for disaster. What can result is often a spiraling down of the partnership, the business and, eventually, a drastic breakup. Jean and her partner could go on as they are, all the while having less of a successful business than they could have if they talked openly.

Keeping things unsaid requires energy. That energy could be redirected into productivity and creativity that could improve both partner's business and personal lives. Many times, clients explain to me that they don't want a confrontation and that is the reason they are not honest about an issue. The irony is that by avoiding a candid early discussion about it, they are setting themselves up for an inevitable confrontation. Eventually, something will cause them to explode and a true confrontation will ensue. Conversely, when the annoyance, objection or disagreement is addressed immediately and calmly, at that point it is not a battle; it is a simple disagreement up for resolution. If there is goodwill between the partners, they will find a way to resolve it or call in a third party expert who is objective and able to facilitate the difficult conversation. In most instances that I have coached, disagreements lose their punch much easier than expected when they are out in the open. Things loom larger and more negative when they are left to fester.

ESSENTIAL QUESTIONS: *Is there anything you are avoiding talking about to your partner or someone else that is weighing heavily on you and adversely affecting your life? This principle is not just for your business partner, but for all relationships in your life. Care enough to free yourself and others who are important to you by talking about what is bothering you . . . now! In the above scenario, would you have been brave enough as either one of these partners to put the issue on the table for discussion?*

Specific Topics That Should be Addressed with Your Partner

How transparent should you be with your potential partner? Obviously, on a first date you are not going to share much personal information, and that is why time spent building the relationship is critical. You each need to be willing to be totally honest in divulging information about those aspects of your life that will affect the business and that you would not necessarily share with a stranger. So, the goal is to be as transparent as you would be with the person you marry; in fact, there may even be more points to talk about, since there are so many aspects to a business. "Transparent" means that you can see through to the other side. It means that there are no curtains up anywhere. Discuss as much as you can before you "plan the wedding."

Below are the main things that you should be able to speak openly about with each other. Start by spending time on your own answering them. You might wonder how you can ask such personal yet essential questions of someone. Generally, it's easier to start by offering your information first; then your partner will feel more comfortable following suit. You can also point to expert advice about how to have a successful partnership, such as the advice I am giving in this book. Share this book as a reference.

YOUR VISION: Are you both (all) wanting to go in the same direction to the same destination?

THE ROLE THE BUSINESS WILL PLAY IN YOUR LIFE: Do both (all) of you put the business on the same level of priorities? Or is it the main business of one and a hobby for the other(s)?

FINANCES: What is your credit rating? How deeply in debt are you? Do you have enough to live on comfortably and also to invest? Would the bank consider you a good risk for a loan?

SPENDING PROPENSITIES: Are you very cautious, even frugal, and to what degree? Do you spend carelessly? How do you make spending decisions?

RISK TOLERANCE: Does one of you want to grow the business faster than the other? Do you both share the same ideas about investing profits? Do you agree on profit sharing and salary levels for yourselves and employees? Does one of you want to hire more help than the other who prefers the do-it-yourself approach?

FAMILY SUPPORT: Hiring family members can work, but more often it doesn't. Do you each share the same viewpoint on this? Do either of you have family members who are against this partnership or business? Do they support it? Will they interfere?

SPOUSES: When my husband and his potential partner were ready to move ahead; we all met for dinner to give us a chance to know if, as couples, we liked each other and to know if the wives were on board. Fortunately, we all clicked. One important thing that came out of it was that both his wife and I expressed our lack of interest to be involved and would not interfere in decision making or anything else. There was no desire on the parts of our husbands for spouses or other family members to have a part in the business. Other partnerships may have a different approach. Some spouses may not be supportive or have personalities that don't mesh. It may not be crucial at this point but could become problematic in the future. In any event, it would be wise to talk about it up front.

TIP: It is a dangerous mistake to not thoroughly discuss the issue of family support, finalize a clear decision regarding this matter and write it into your agreements.

PERSONAL OBLIGATIONS: It is important to understand where your partner is in his or her personal life. Children, aging parents, family illnesses, divorce, alimony, ongoing support for a family member, mortgages, private schools and colleges all should be discussed so that each partner knows the pressures on the other and how they are dealt with. Are there other responsibilities that would be a distraction, like an already existing business? Is there family support for your business and for the partnership? Is there a spouse who wants to be involved?

HEALTH: Do you or a member of your family have health problems that could interfere with your work schedule or availability? This is not necessarily a deal breaker if you talk about it and plan to make it work in advance.

PREVIOUS WORK HISTORY AND EXPERIENCE: What worked and what didn't? What did you learn?

PREVIOUS BUSINESSES AND PARTNERSHIPS: What worked and what didn't? What did you learn? What was your role in things not working? Did you take responsibility for it or was your partner to blame?

STRENGTHS AND WEAKNESSES: What are yours? What are your partner's?

SKILLS, TALENTS AND INTERESTS: What do you love to do? What do you hate to do? You may be skilled in an area that you don't love doing. Would you do it until you can hire an employee to take over with you managing that area?

ANNOYING TRAITS: What are the things about you that others have found to be annoying or difficult? Be honest; everyone has them.

WORK STYLE: Are you a workaholic or more laid back? If you differ in your work habits, can you accept that about your partner; or, can you somehow compromise?

GOALS AND PRIORITIES: What are your priorities and long-term goals? What is your vision and mission for the business? What is your potential partner's? What brought you to the business? What brought your partner? Was it a lifelong dream, a recent inspiration, a desire to make money or answer a market need or the result of your education?

VALUES AND WORK ETHIC: Do you and your potential partner(s) share core values about treatment of employees and clients? What about your respective families? If one of you is married and the other not, is there understanding and flexibility about priorities? Do you share a value and strategy about giving back to the community?

When talking out the above points, bear in mind that differences between you may be subtle, so keep the discussion going to reveal them. In doing so, you will also be creating a communication style that will continue to work for you in the future. In other cases, as the following case study emphasizes, disparities in what each of you want out of the partnership may be revealed, even between two people who know each other very well.

Partners Must be on the Same Page from the Beginning

Two of my clients are brothers who have always been close. They liked each other and got along well. One day, they had an idea for an Internet-based business. When I asked each of them to tell me their long-term vision, Bob said that he'd like it to be a success in a couple of years and sell it for top dollar. Bill looked at him in surprise and added that his intention was to make it successful and hand it over to his children. The good news is that they put this difference on the table at the outset, rather than one day Bob shocking his brother with his desire to sell. Knowing this in advance allowed them to plan an appropriate exit strategy.

That's the point of dating: you put things on the table up front in order to discover not just compatibility but incompatibility. Don't assume that you are thinking the same thing just because you both have the same enthusiasm for opening this business and know each other as well as these brothers. Educate yourself so that you can avert disasters down the road.

TIP: Don't assume that because most everything so far seems the same between you, that everything else will be. If you haven't discussed it, you are making an assumption. Put it on the table and check it out.

ESSENTIAL QUESTION: *Were you ever surprised to discover something that was very different about someone else whom you had previously thought you knew well?*

Sometimes, values that were in place at the startup phase can change due to unforeseen circumstances. Here's an example.

Partnerships Can End When Values Change

Frank and Conrad had been in a partnership for 10 years selling financial products. They both had strong shared values about keeping clients in safe investments. Then the economy took a downturn and business dropped off significantly. Conrad took some courses with a wirehouse whose products carried more risk than they were comfortable with, but Conrad saw the possibility of building up their company's income if they went that route. Frank remained uncomfortable with this drastic change in values about protecting their clients.

They saw me for one session and it became clear that Frank had remained true to their original mission while Conrad was taking another road entirely. Consequently, they made the decision to end the partnership. Fortunately, they had a buy-sell agreement as the first step in their exit strategy, and were able to put it into action parting amicably.

ESSENTIAL QUESTIONS: *When is the last time you and your partner talked about your visions and values? Are there differences between you? Do you try to resolve them? Compromise? Live with them? Are they written down?*

Are Complementary Skills Required?

Common wisdom dictates that partners must have complementary skills in order to create a successful business. My experience as a coach tells me otherwise. While it may be useful, even ideal, to have different strengths that parallel each other and round out the partners' skill set, it can be equally helpful when both partners have the same skills. After all, two heads are better than one, and when brainstorming, no matter the skills brought to the table, multiple viewpoints about the same issue will offer multiple possibilities. I have seen partnerships in which both people met in the same learning environment, learning and loving the same skills, even having similar talents, not complementary ones. The result was high-level brainstorming and collaboration. Even partners who have complementary skills are still likely to need additional people to cover skill sets that neither of them possess and, as a result, will hire someone else to do those tasks.

By way of example, Sylvia and Charlotte are manufacturers of fashionable and functional diaper bags who took the same classes in product design, production and marketing. They are very similar in skill level and talents, and both enjoy doing the same things together. They don't have complementary skills, but they complemented each other by brainstorming ideas that are better than either of them could come up with on their own. The result is a line of fabulous designs that have helped their company grow at a brisk pace.

ESSENTIAL QUESTIONS: *Conventional wisdom is often wrong. Do you agree? What out-of-the-ordinary way of doing something have you experienced? How did it work for you?*

Google is a powerful example of a successful partnership in which the founders' skills are not complementary. Larry Page grew up in Michigan and Sergey Brin is from Russia. Both had a passion for computers at a young age. They founded Google in 1998, after they'd met just three years earlier in Stanford University's PhD program. As the story goes, Page and Brin didn't become instant friends; in fact, during a campus tour for doctoral students, Brin was Page's guide and they bickered the entire time. Yet as fate would have it, the two found themselves working together on a research project. The result of that project was their paper, titled "The Anatomy of a Large-Scale Hypertextual Web Search Engine." That research became the basis for Google. Despite not having complementary skills, what makes their partnership work? They bonded over their passion for data mining and their shared vision for their company.

Keep Dating and Keep Asking Questions

The added benefits of the dating process beyond learning about each other is that you develop a comfortable mode of communicating which, with practice, keeps improving. If you find it difficult to open up to one another and be transparent as this process moves forward, you might be wise to walk away now. If transparency and trust still seem difficult after having these discussions, consider hiring a coach. Without a concerted effort to iron things out early on, it's not going to get easier later when the business becomes more complex.

Now is the time to add more questions to the list we've already reviewed. Make notes about what you are learning and what concerns you still have. Before concluding that you will be good partners, ask yourselves:

- Is trust and respect for your potential partner(s) increasing? Are you friends beyond the scope of your business? If so, how? If not, how does that feel? (Note: friendship outside of business is not a requirement for success.)
- If this business doesn't fly, is your relationship good enough that you would want to try a different business with this partner? If yes, do you have other ideas in mind?

***

After a sufficient courtship, you will feel more confident that you've either found your best business partner match or not. The most important thing is to find out as much as possible about your potential partner and reveal as much of yourself to your partner, as well. Openness and understanding will ensure that you create a solid foundational match. As long as expectations and understandings are clear from the beginning and are planned for—and if there is good will and clear, reasonable expectations between the partners—you will be starting off on the right foot.

Chapter 4
All in the Family: Partnering with Friends, Spouses and Relatives

"A friendship founded on business is a good deal better than a business founded on friendship."

–John D. Rockefeller

Clients often ask me if it is a good idea to form a business partnership with friends, relatives or spouses. My answer is usually "maybe," as it depends on whether or not they have completed the steps that I am outlining here. Although you already know the person, I recommend following the same process as if you are just getting to know this "potential business partner" for the first time.

Working with someone whom you already know in your personal life has its appeal, of course. You may already be aware of each other's quirks, habits, interests and feelings about family, politics, work and personal time. You are generally comfortable with one another. That said, simply being familiar with someone does not mean that you know how they would feel, think and behave in a business setting—and particularly, not specifically in a business partnership with you. Don't make the mistake of skipping the dating phase or any of the other critical foundational work.

In any business partnership, partnership agreements play a vital role. In order to help ensure success when partnering with someone you know (the same as if your partner was not previously known to you), it is imperative that you write a clear agreement. Many friends, spouses, lovers and family members may not want to face the fact that negatives may arise and because of this timidity, they forgo writing an agreement. (We will cover this subject in Part II.)

Treat this process with the same respect, even if you know your partners well. Actually, when you believe that you know someone well, you are more likely to make erroneous assumptions about where they stand or how they would react in a crisis. Clarifying and strengthening your relationship even more is still the key to success. The following stories illustrate some of the unique situations that arise as a result of partnering with friends, relatives or a spouse.

Working with Relatives: How Do You Fire Mom?

This case study about Cathy and Stephanie is not uncommon. It was convenient to have Stefanie's mother be their bookkeeper for their children's photography

DOI 10.1515/9781547400188-004

studio when they were starting out on a shoestring budget, because neither Cathy nor she were suited to do it and Mom was happy to help without being paid. However, nearing the end of their first somewhat successful year of being partners, Mom was giving financial advice without being asked and making decisions about spending without consulting them. She enjoyed having a place to go every day and was in the studio more often than was warranted. She had opinions about everything and didn't wait to be asked for them.

Stefanie wasn't happy about all of this, but wasn't willing to fire Mom or even set acceptable limits for her involvement. Cathy became increasingly outraged. The two of them, who started out well together, now barely spoke and when they did, it usually ended in a shouting match. Eventually, the partnership was over and the only good thing was that Stefanie was able to buy Cathy's share. Without Cathy, Stefanie and her mother continued the business together. Had they written into their agreement a policy that no family members were to be hired, Stefanie would have been able to thank her mother for volunteering before they had money to pay a bookkeeper, and referring to their written decision about not hiring family members, it could have been easy.

ESSENTIAL QUESTIONS: *Do you have strong feelings one way or another about including family members in your business? Do you know if your partner(s) shares the same opinion? If not, how will you resolve it or will you end up like Stefanie and Cathy?*

The following case study involves a tricky partnership configuration—a family business that includes a father, two sons and a friend. Read on to learn how they made it all work.

Working as a Team Makes This Partnership Work

E-HELP Enterprises, Inc. is a company with three subsidiaries. One manages solely family owned entities, and the other two raise funds from non-family investors and acquire real estate and private equity assets. The company is owned by Harvey Knell and his wife, Ellen (who does not work in the business). Peter and Lorin Knell, two of their three sons, do work in the business, along with an MBA classmate of Lorin's, Bob Blair. They share equal status as managing partners, receive similar compensation and they all (in addition to Harvey Knell) constitute the Investment Committee. Peter focuses primarily on the real estate activities, and Lorin and Bob focus primarily on the private equity activities.

They work as a team, however, and if a vote to move on a deal is not unanimous among the four of them, they abandon it. A number of other things make this atypical family business partnership work. One is their shared ethics and values on how to treat their clients, each other, their employees and joint venture partners. Fairness is their measure. They also have total trust in one another and respect for each other's skills. Nothing is left without a discussion. All issues are put on the table and talked about until resolved. Conflicts are rare and they were hard pressed to come up with an example to the contrary when I asked them for one.

Peter and Lorin are the two younger brothers and have always gotten along. They have similar temperaments and like each other, spending time outside of work on a soccer team and in other ways. All three of the partners are fathers of young children from six months to 12 years of age, and they understand the need for each to sometimes take extra time for family, which is a value that all of them share. They accept each other's different work styles. All three work long hours, sometimes from home, and whenever needed, morning, noon or night. Harvey implicitly trusts the three of them to make decisions when he is out of town.

ESSENTIAL QUESTIONS: *How do you compare with your partner(s) regarding shared ethics, values, trust, respect, flexibility and ability to talk about everything as it may occur and prevent conflicts? Do either of you tend to blame the other, and for what?*

Best Friends as Business Partners

I read the story of a partnership between two best friends, Jenny Silbert and Lisa Siedlecki, in the *Larchmont Chronicle*, a monthly newspaper in Larchmont Village, Los Angeles. I was intrigued by their story and asked if they'd agree to be interviewed. Their company, Rewilder (rewilder.com), repurposes post-industrial materials that would otherwise end up in a landfill. They use the material to manufacture a variety of attractive and useful handbags.

Jenny is married and the mother of two young children who require attention, while Lisa is currently single. Their close friendship culminated in a business partnership. Both gave up high salaried positions in the corporate world to pursue their present mission of effecting positive change for the environment through design. The two are so in sync that one practically knows what the other is thinking—but that doesn't mean they are the same person. One challenge that they face with each other is differences in their work styles. Jenny prefers a task list on the wall with due dates. This is important for her to understand tasks and manage time. Lisa prefers that everything just flow, knowing that in the end it gets done on time. They are mapping out a compromise by scheduling major milestones and managing everyday tasks separately.

What makes their partnership work so well is their commitment, ongoing communication, trust and concern for each other. They respect each other's expertise and listen to the other's instincts on new ideas; if they both don't like something, they don't do it. Because of a deep regard for one another, they are dedicated to making their business, partnership and friendship work—with the friendship taking top priority.

ESSENTIAL QUESTIONS: *Without such a deep friendship do you think this partnership would work, considering that one partner has family obligations and the other doesn't? Are these keys to success starting to sound familiar?*

The following friendship example found where to draw the line before it was too late.

A Friendship Saved

Thomas made his living buying fixer-uppers and flipping them in their newly renovated state. His best friend, Robert, wanted to join him on some of the projects. They had been friends since high school, long before each of them married. Thomas and Robert enjoyed working out together at the local gym and played poker with a group of friends every week. They often spent time together with their wives and children.

So, Thomas agreed to let Robert join him in the next house he was considering buying. Following the purchase, Thomas began dealing with the contractor to make investment decisions about the repairs and upgrades. Robert was present for these conversations and at first stood by just listening. There was some beginning tension as Robert felt that he had no part in the project except for putting up half of the money. Eventually, he spoke up with ideas and options, but they were not in keeping with Thomas' budget and experience. He was insistent and Thomas, out of respect for letting him have some say, agreed to some of his suggestions.

The outcome was that they earned less than planned on the sale. Thomas called me for a quick strategy session to resolve the crisis that was threatening the partnership. It was easy to recognize how vulnerable their friendship had become in this business arrangement. Thomas decided to tell Robert (who was thinking the same thing, by the way) that it was far more important to remain friends than to be partners in business. They agreed to not do any further business together and reverted to being friends only.

ESSENTIAL QUESTIONS: *Would you have sought help at the time that Thomas did? Would you have allowed the tension to build? Would you have argued with Robert or given in as Thomas did even though he knew the business and that Robert's ideas were not going to help? Would you have backed off if you were Robert or insisted on having your opinions honored?*

Sometimes, partnership breakups become the stuff of legends. One even made it into the plot of a feature Hollywood film, *The Social Network*, in 2010. Unless you've been living under a rock, you've heard about the fallout between the two Facebook founders Mark Zuckerberg and Eduardo Saverin. The former college buddies developed the original Facebook while they were undergrads at Harvard University. According to the Hollywood depiction, Saverin was forced out of the company, thanks to a betrayal on the part of Zuckerberg. However, closer inspection suggests that Zuckerberg elected to try and cut Saverin out of the company for a number of fairly valid reasons, including that Eduardo had allegedly been using Facebook as a free ad platform for his own project. The pair settled in 2009, with Saverin reducing his stake in Facebook from over 30 percent to 5. Now based in Singapore, Saverin says that he harbors no ill feeling towards Zuckerberg.

Married Partners: Saying "I Do" Twice

It probably comes as no surprise that not all married couples can work together in business. In fact, most probably wouldn't do well in this type of professional situation. Married partners face what others don't in that all the trials and tribulations of the business are easily brought home in a double dose. It can even be more than double if a child or children work in the business. Although my parents weren't business partners, my mother worked as my father's secretary for many years. Even that was a challenge given their totally opposite work styles. Both had strong personalities with opinions to match.

So when it comes to partnering with a spouse, a few extra tips will come in handy to help you delineate between being life partners and business partners. Since it's extremely easy to get wrapped up in the business, the marriage itself may begin to show signs of wear and tear. One of the best ways to help ensure that you make time for your marriage and your business is to set clear boundaries as to what is "work time" and what is "married time." Although this may sound structured and unromantic, setting and upholding these boundaries can help prevent communication and relationship disruptions.

Schedule regular business meetings during business hours that do not impinge on family time and yet are needed to keep you both in the know. Below are two stories of successful married partners who do exactly that—they separate business and married time. As you read their stories, note the significant commonalities between them and others you've read about in previous chapters. Then ask yourself where you stand in relation to them. Let's begin with the Lessers, who established a simple rule that keeps their successful business relationship and family time separate.

One Sentence Changed the Business

Linda Lesser is in the real estate business with her husband, Michael, and son, Tim. Their company, The Lessers (thelessers.com) is a member of Keller Williams Realty in Encino, California. Linda offers the following advice that she says was a turning point for their business. She advises spouses to find the courage to be open and honest with each other.

One day, about two years into the business partnership, something happened on the way to a client meeting. Driving in the car, she turned to Michael, who had brought up a personal matter.

"I'm not your spouse right now," Linda said. "I am your business partner and we can discuss this later."

From that moment on, "everything changed." Now, business is business and they are each free to let the other know there is an issue that will be discussed after business hours. Tim learned by watching his parents and respects the same boundaries. The Lessers' story points out that it's important for family members to distinguish that business is business, no matter what the family issue is at the moment—short of a true emergency.

ESSENTIAL QUESTIONS: *Are both of you open enough to express your true feelings as they come up and discuss them comfortably and lovingly? Do you respect each other in business? Do either of you acquiesce to the other's judgment regularly? Does one of you always give in?*

This next couple, my clients Sydney Weisman and David Hamlin, work out of their home, which intensifies the challenge of being married to your business partner.

Keep Business and Married Time Separate

Sydney and David own Weisman Hamlin Public Relations (whpr.com), a successful Los Angeles firm that focuses primarily on nonprofit public relations and advocacy campaigns. They were concerned that the amount of business they were doing did not reflect the level of their capabilities and expertise. Some probing revealed that since they had a good marriage that was indicative of their love for each other, they tended not to set expectations for each other beyond each of their comfort zones. That has changed over the years. As I coached them through this, we also addressed the boundaries between business and married time, and setting regularly scheduled meeting times for "business only" topics. For this book, I recently asked them for specific tips that have been working best for them. They offered these three:

1. Do business during business hours then close the doors. Do the same for vacation time.
2. Have enormous respect for each other's talents. Rely on the strengths of each other and recognize that together the sum is greater.
3. Schedule regular business meetings where the discussion is about how to better serve clients, and future goals and plans.

ESSENTIAL QUESTIONS: *Are you and your spouse on the same page regarding boundaries? Does one or both of you constantly cross them? Do you and your spouse feel that your worth to the business is equal? Where do you most often disagree? Do you keep business disagreements out of your marriage time?*

Married Business Partners Defy the Odds

I met LaMae Weber because we are both board members of The People Concern, a nonprofit organization that provides beds and services to the mentally ill homeless in Los Angeles. When I learned that she and her husband, Nami Ataee, are partners in the digital marketing agency Dream Warrior (DreamWarrior. com), I wanted to know more and was graciously granted an interview.

By all standards, the business partnership relationship between LaMae and Nami should not be working as well as it is. They have completely different backgrounds, as well as distinct temperaments and work styles. Nami says that LaMae is trusting, comes from her heart and is willing to take time to find a way to make something work. She ponders the consequences before deciding to give up on someone or something. LaMae uses the word "impulsive" to describe Nami's decision making, which he says makes good sense because he makes decisions based on numbers. Nami considers himself to be more pragmatic. He is much less trusting of people than LaMae.

What has not just kept them together but makes their partnership and their business thrive is a number of things, but their big secret is to throw a healthy dose of humor into the mix and laugh at themselves. When they disagree, which is not an unusual occurrence, it may be loud but it's never accompanied with anger. More than that, they both recognize the value that the other brings and are willing to listen to each other.

They have 12 employees locally and 10 across the globe. Their shared ethics and core values are to treat their employees and clients with respect and honesty. In 2006, they engaged a coach once a month to help with strategy and communication between them. Their business has had double-digit sales increases every year since then.

ESSENTIAL QUESTION: *What elements does this partnership share as keys to success that other successful partnerships also do?*

Sharing your work life with a spouse, friend or family member does call for some creative thinking and a strong commitment to maintain boundaries. As with all of life, your business is subject to changing circumstances. If you find that your boundaries are becoming blurred, revamp your strategies. Call a meeting with your partner and do just that.

***

As you can see, going into partnership with someone you know—a friend, relative or spouse—is certainly no guarantee that everything will be smooth sailing, even if the collaboration is successful for many years. So it's still important to thoroughly evaluate what your working relationship will be.

Once you have decided that you and your potential partner(s) have become sufficiently acquainted and know that this is a good fit (whether it's someone you don't know well, or a best friend or relative), it is time to move on to the next step: making a decision to create that partnership. Before flipping to the next chapter, though, double-check your decision by using the following questions to help you evaluate just a bit further (or, to fortify your existing partnership).

— Do you and your partner(s) have the skills that you each sought or are you in agreement about filling in or hiring others?

— Have you shared your reasons for wanting the business?

— What more have you learned about where your personalities or work styles collide?

- Have you found yourselves to be in sync on the most important issues? Are you able to compromise where you are not?
- Are you now sure that you are equally passionate about the business? If not, how will that play out?
- Are your visions still the same or compatible?
- Are you double-checking your shared core values/ethics? Have you translated them into your mission statement?
- Do your spouses/families support this business and the partnership?
- Are you open with each other and communicate easily?
- Are you both willing to adapt, reevaluate and modify as things progress? Have you made some strategic decisions about how you will do this?
- Have you begun talking about how you will resolve disagreements?
- Have you begun to think about an exit strategy?
- Are you meeting on a regularly scheduled basis that will continue and expand?
- Has your relationship progressed to the point that you have respect and concern for each other's wellbeing?
- Do you like each other and enjoy spending time together?

Chapter 5
Take a Vow or Walk Away: Deciding to Move Forward or Not

"After mutual respect and understanding are achieved, it is possible to establish real, sincere relationships, which is the foundation of a solid long-term collaboration."

–Ron Garan, astronaut and author of
*The Orbital Perspective: Lessons in Seeing the
Big Picture from a Journey of 71 Million Miles*

Vanessa and Valerie, each in their early twenties, had all the bells and whistles in place for a seemingly perfect partnership. They had similar businesses in the skin care industry, each with a modicum of success, and they had complementary skills. Valerie created products and sold them on the Internet and at home parties, while Vanessa had a newsletter about health and beauty that reached thousands of subscribers each month. It seemed like a fabulous idea for them to partner up.

Fortunately, they had already spent a couple of months "dating" and knew enough about each other to realize that becoming partners seemed to be a reasonable outcome. But despite their desire to make it work, as the weeks went on, they began to discover issues that they couldn't resolve on their own. In the process of drawing up a partnership agreement, their lawyer suggested that they see me first. The difficulties they encountered were centered around their unwillingness to relinquish their self-interests in favor of the good of the business.

Valerie felt that she deserved a greater portion of the money and the title of CEO due to the fact that she was contributing the actual patented products. Vanessa believed that she deserved a larger sum of money because she had a following, was contributing more of the finances and would be responsible for sales and marketing. She also wanted to top the hierarchy as the CEO. They both held fast to their opinions and it became obvious that each was only looking at what they could gain from the partnership and not what they could give.

In our coaching sessions, we talked about possible compromises, to which there was agreement at the moment, but by the time our next session came up, they each had reverted to their original positions. Mistrust and lack of respect for each other had begun to infiltrate and taint the process. After four coaching sessions, I concluded that this relationship was not meant to be. Although disappointed and a little angry at me for not "fixing it," fortunately, they paid attention and walked away before it was too late. As "the coach who didn't fix it," I felt

DOI 10.1515/9781547400188-005

quite satisfied that our time together saved them from a contentious relationship and costly breakup down the road.

Vanessa and Valerie's experience is a good example of a potential partnership story with a happy ending that may not have seemed happy at the time. While their inability to proceed with the partnership may have been dubbed a failure by outsiders, it was actually a best-case scenario given the circumstances. Potential partners who are unable or unwilling to work through their differences will be in jeopardy. This will become apparent almost immediately or at some point in the future of the business.

The high statistics of failure point to potential partners ignoring their own intuitive knowledge or "gut feelings" that something is not right. Too often, potential partners are so eager to find a partner and roll out the business that they ignore their own best judgment and red flags fluttering right in front of their faces. They move ahead in wishful thinking mode. This illogical and harmful way of proceeding generally leads to disastrous outcomes, and accounts for the high rate of partnership failure.

If dating your potential partner brought you to the conclusion that you are not meant for each other, rather than wallowing in disappointment, feel grateful to have found this out before actually going through with the partnership. Save yourselves the misery and expense of a breakup. Shake hands, say goodbye and walk away now before it has the possibility of becoming anything on the continuum of "less than amicable" to "tragically destructive." When partnerships dissolve, other people often take the side of one or the other partner. Partners on the brink of breaking up can cause great strife in their surroundings. Don't allow things to come to this.

ESSENTIAL QUESTIONS: *Is there anything in a partner or partnership that would be a deal breaker for you? What are your must-haves? Make a list and think about them deeper, and then from your partner's point of view. Is there anything you would overlook in order to have a partner in this business? Is that wisdom or desperation?*

A Model Partnership . . . Again and Again

The ideal choice of a partner is one with whom you'd want to partner again if, for whatever reason, your present business ends. Larry Flax and Rick Rosenfield are a terrific example. They are co-founders of the popular restaurant chain California Pizza Kitchen, or CPK as it's affectionately known. They graciously granted me an interview when I learned that prior to upstarting CPK, Flax and Rosenfield had become friends as colleagues—first as assistant US attorneys, then in 1973 as partners in a law firm, which they left to create their own law firm, Flax and Rosenfield.

They opened CPK, their second official partnership, in 1985 and jointly ran the company until they sold it in 2011. While Larry searched the globe for another business venture, Rick enjoyed taking time off to golf and fish. Early in 2014, they joined forces for a third time to develop a new restaurant concept.

Flax and Rosenfield's partnership relationship is a model template for how to choose so well that you will always want to partner together in subsequent businesses. They say that their main "glue" is trust. Neither of them ever had reason to question the other's loyalty, ethics or honesty. (I can't stress enough that if a partnership—either business or personal—doesn't have these three essential characteristics, it won't endure.)

Interestingly, Larry and Rick say they each have healthy, intact egos and often have different points of view, but neither is invested in being right. Their experience as lawyers taught them to listen to all sides of an argument and so listening and being open to another opinion is who they are. They shared one of their favorite sayings with me, "Just because you are certain doesn't mean you're right." They claim to have never said to each other, "you are wrong." They always find a way to reach an agreement. They couldn't think of a disagreement to tell me about because they always keep discussing an issue until they reach a consensus. Laughingly, Rick brought up Larry's idea of having egg salad pizza on the menu as their worst failure. The loss was a few tubs of egg salad, he said.

Yet the synergy between them is more than the glue of trust. They know that they are much better off together than not, that "one plus one equals three" in their case. They agree on how failure in partnerships often starts: when one person believes he is more important to the partnership than the other.

ESSENTIAL QUESTIONS: *What are the must haves for success that Larry and Rick demonstrate? How different or similar are they to other successful partnerships? What are the specific similarities?*

***

So, you've gotten to know each other, you've had a sufficient courtship and you've asked each other some tough, in-depth questions. How do you know if it's ultimately right to move forward or cut bait? Make sure you have realistically assessed all aspects of this dating period. Don't move ahead just because you want it more than you want to note any red flags. If your intuition is telling you this is not right, pay attention, shake hands and move on. By the same token, if all has gone well, and you honestly share mutual trust, respect, openness and good communication—as well as share values and vision for the business—then kudos! It's time to make it official.

If you have not done so already, you should download the free *Guide to Choosing the Right Partner* available on the Product page at www.bizpartner.com.

Part II: **Planning for Your Future Together**

Chapter 6
Setting a Solid Foundation: The BPAT

"Everyone has a responsibility to not only tolerate another person's point of view, but also to accept it eagerly as a challenge to your own understanding."
–Arlo Guthrie

So, you've made the decision to walk down the aisle towards business partnership bliss. This is an exciting time! Shared creative adrenaline has birthed a potential partnership and it's blooming into a beautiful thing. Everything is moving along quickly now and you're ready to get on with building the business together.

As you proceed, continue to work on communication and trust building. This starry-eyed honeymoon phase is also when unforeseen annoyances may begin to appear. There is the occasional mishap: Someone forgets to call the telephone company or run software updates. Personality traits begin to show themselves more clearly: someone has a tendency to procrastinate or emerges as a workaholic. Because you only want to be happy and secure in your decision, you blow off these minor aggravations in an effort to get along and not sweat the small stuff. While noble, always taking the high road in this way can eventually lead to bigger problems down the line. Express yourself openly, honestly and respectfully in this newlywed business phase, just as you would at any other time. Continue to listen to that inner voice and talk about every issue on the spot, or as soon as possible.

Keep in mind that having differing opinions is a good thing. It means that each partner is engaged and wanting to keep the business moving. If these differences are discussed when they occur, they can most often be worked out long before there is trouble in paradise. They will only become full-on conflicts when: 1) the commitment to the partnership is less than 100% or 2) the differences have been overlooked and given time to fester.

As you continue to lay the foundation for your fledgling partnership, this is also the time to handle a few essentials: formalizing the partnership and your mutual business goals on paper. This includes the completion of the four documents that I have found to be absolutely imperative:

1. **Business Partnership Agreement Template, or BPAT**. The BPAT is the most important document to solidify your partnership relationship and create a strong foundation for your business.   In this chapter I will supply you with enough information to create your own BPAT or you can purchase the original BPAT which I wrote (see the Introduction for details).   The BPAT, I wrote expertly guides your conversations to create, maintain and

DOI 10.1515/9781547400188-006

strengthen the foundation of your business partnership relationship, preparing you for day-to-day functioning, unexpected events or roadblocks, through to a win/win exit strategy. You will be guided to skillfully have the difficult conversations, decide on a method to resolve conflicts and to answer questions you never thought about asking. I created it because I could see where partnerships were repeatedly running into trouble, and subsequently how to prevent misunderstandings, eliminate wrong assumptions and memory lapses, and instill clear decision-making among the partners. The BPAT was born out of my singular desire to help partners clarify and solidify their relationships, which will help them avoid a big part of the reason why 70% of them fail.

2. A **Partnership Agreement, or PA,** drawn up by a lawyer, will be discussed in Chapter 8.
3. **A Business Plan** for your new enterprise. (We will cover this in Chapter 9.)
4. **"What If" scenario planning**. I have also created an original document called the *What If Scenario Handbook to Prepare for the Unexpected Before It Occurs*, (free with the purchase of the *Business Partnership Agreement Template*), so that partners can anticipate unforeseen circumstances that might arise down the road, and thereby plan for them. This will be discussed in more detail in Chapter 10.

The good news is that all of the due diligence you have done with vetting your partner(s) will prove its value in this stage of the process, as the information you've learned about each other will be the content you will now formalize in these written agreements and other planning documents. Do not procrastinate on any of these steps. The health of your future partnership greatly depends on following through with all this information. Taking care to complete all these documents will go far to secure your partnership and protect your dream. So, let's get on with it. I will walk you through each of these critical documents, one by one in subsequent chapters.

TIP: The best policy is to spell everything out on paper.

The Business Partnership Agreement Template

First, let's review the most important document of all, the Business Partnership Agreement Template. The BPAT will solidify your relationship by covering everything about how you will operate the business. It is the major tool to prevent most conflicts. The secret to getting the distribution of work right for long-term success is in the way you set it up at the very beginning. Too many partnerships get into trouble eventually, with bad feelings, blame and self-righteous declarations that "I'm doing more than my share and my partner isn't doing what he said he would."

This common scenario can be completely avoided if enough time is invested to think through everything and record it in the BPAT. Whatever the time and energy you devote to this process is a pittance compared to the cost that arguments and disagreements will have on the functioning of the business.

The most frequent calls I receive from partners are cries for help, indicating that a rescue is needed. When these calls do come in, I often hear an angry, exasperated person on the other end of the line who is complaining that the other partner is not doing the work that he or she promised to do. These individuals will often offer me great detail about the work he or she has to do to cover for the inept partner. Seldom is this picture of the situation accurate, but I know as I listen that the anger and despair are symptoms of deeper, ongoing and unaddressed issues among the partners.

So, what is the solution? The partners need to go back and talk about all of the points in the BPAT, starting with their original vision for the business. With this document as a guide, their conversations can address all of the areas of the company's structure, how they each work in it and how they work with each other. Once partners make decisions about each issue, they should record their findings into what is now a well-thought-out document that is unique and personal to them. The results of this process are enhanced communication, a reaffirmation of trust and a reinvigorated sense of each partner's interest and goals for the business. The bottom line will reflect these actions in a positive way, as well.

Drafting the BPAT

Begin by brainstorming every detail of your business. (Later you will also enter some of this information into your business plan.) Be guided by your vision and mission statements, and your strategic plan (more about these items in a minute), and come up with all the functions that the business needs. Be as specific as possible.

Next, get personal. What are the strengths, skills, talents, likes and dislikes of each partner? What is each of your areas of expertise and what do you most enjoy doing? Using these criteria, everyone can have dibs on being in charge of, for example, finance, sales, design or technology. Three possibilities may occur here:

1. More than one person may prefer the same area.
2. No partner wants or has any expertise in a given but necessary area.
3. One person is perfectly suited and is happy to take on an area of the business.

In the first scenario, some resolution, compromise or a coin toss may be used. In the second, either someone agrees to do what they don't know or like well, at least for the time being or until they can afford to hire someone to do it, or hire now. The partner in charge of a particular area, such as finance, may or may not actually do the tasks required but would be accountable for overseeing that they are done by someone. Too often, partners focus their attention primarily on the area of their charge while assuming that others are doing the same. Then a day comes when a crisis occurs, such as the loss of a major client, investments that have gone sour, a bad decision by one partner regarding inventory, or partners who have generally lost sight of their original vision. So, please note this very important point: The partner who is not in charge of a particular area does not have a pass on his or her responsibilities for the business as a whole; therefore, this person has to be in the know about the big picture at all times. I've included a number of stories on these pages where this advice was not heeded, and you will be able to see what brought the partnership down.

TIP: If the conversation becomes emotional or difficult for any reason, invest in a session or two with a coach to facilitate. The return on investment can be saving your partnership relationship and your business.

As previously mentioned, the BPAT guides you through discussions that you had in the dating period about your vision, mission, values, goals and more. The difference here is that these get addressed and confirmed on a deeper even more committed level as you clarify and write them into the document. One of the most important aspects (and saving grace to your relationship) of the BPAT is that you will be deciding, based on the skills of each, who will be responsible for what area of the business, how conflicts will be resolved, and what the strategy will be for planned or unplanned exits. I've stated this earlier and will say it again for emphasis: discussions that you have for completing the BPAT should be honest, open, friendly and clarifying in order to avoid misunderstandings, forgetfulness and making incorrect assumptions. Keep in mind that this is all about the business. The partners are parts of the machine that makes it work. It's up to each of you to commit to do whatever is necessary for the good of the company, whether or not one of you spends more time than the other(s).

An added bonus to completing the BPAT is a deepening of your partnership relationship even further and putting in place a true mode of communication that will be ongoing. Your written agreement will act as the cement that will hold your desires and business goals in place. And many of the decisions in it can now be used in your legal partnership agreement (which I will discuss next), so you have saved some of the hourly costs with a lawyer.

Writing It Down Can Save Anguish in the Future

Desiree and Linda had a great business idea: an event planning venture that encompassed weddings, retirement parties, adult birthday parties and the like, preceded by each woman having been successful in their respective previous businesses. They tried hard to create their partnership so that it would be a success, but as they spoke to me about it, I came to understand that a trusting relationship didn't exist. Desiree was hung up on how much time she spent each day doing her end of the work, primarily designing and setting up each party, as opposed to the time Linda spent on her work, which was sales and marketing. A variety of details upon which they disagreed did nothing but make moving ahead impossible.

Eight months into it, the business they had started with enthusiasm was quickly crumbling. They had different levels of commitment to one another, and their bond was eroding. A lack of regard, respect and trust was evident. When they spoke to me about the business, I felt the pretense of politeness, cooperation and concern, but I could see clearly that each one had one foot out the door already. When I brought this to their attention, neither would admit to being insincere in her commitment to the business or the other partner. True commitment, I told them, means you don't have the tiniest of safeguards that allow you to keep one foot out the door, which means you don't have a true commitment. Instead, you stay the course until you have worked out your differences or a solution that is a win-win for everyone.

In our work together, I helped them admit that theirs was not the best match and to face the fact that their enthusiasm for the partnership and the business was diminishing rapidly. The good news is that they were responsive to ending it according to the exit strategy they had in place in their partnership agreement. They had spelled out who owns what, how they would divide assets after all the bills were paid, how they could each continue their previous businesses without competing, and that neither would be allowed to use the business name.

ESSENTIAL QUESTIONS: *Trust can be tricky. Are you trustworthy in your situation or do you only pay lip service to it? Is your partner truly trustworthy? Are you each just playing a role because you'd like it to work?*

Finances, spending patterns, personal debt, and risk tolerance are a major foundation for your partnership, so be sure your BPAT and partnership agreement covers these areas in depth. Creating the BPAT calls for partners to ask themselves and each other a series of searching questions and then answer them honestly. What would happen in the future should one partner lose enthusiasm and wish to sell the business? Who is actually responsible for what? How will disputes that arise be resolved? Merging two visions into one is, at best, as precarious and difficult as walking a tightrope.

Again, don't believe those who say emotions don't belong in business; they do. Your emotions matter and will be revealed in the midst of conversations—in your body language, words chosen, facial expressions and overall responses to your partner and how you feel inside yourself. Be honest with yourself in the process of being honest with your partner about your business. As the following story and the others you've read so far have shown, quality communication is the main essential.

BPAT Saves the Business

Rachel complained that she was doing all the work in her photography business. She felt that her partner, Carl, was not fulfilling his end of the bargain, since he was so often missing from the scene. This complaint between partners is common, but rarely is one partner's description of the situation the way it actually is. In this case, Rachel's impression took hold, as misunderstandings often do, because she and Carl hadn't been communicating and she didn't really know what Carl was spending his time doing. Rachel and Carl both admitted that it had been a long time since they had met to talk about their business. They had no prior written agreement.

Rachel was in charge of sales and marketing, while Carl handled the finances and equipment. Late in the game, Rachel became aware that some of Carl's financial decisions were not in accord with her best judgment. Because of their history together and commitment to the business, in their first coaching session with me, they agreed to look at the steps they had skipped and acknowledge the need for ongoing communication in regular meetings, which they now agreed to institute. I suggested that they start with putting together a partnership agreement using my BPAT then take that information to an attorney to draw up a legal partnership agreement. They were able to do this without further coaching. When I spoke with them to check on their progress, they were thrilled to see how both their relationship and the business had improved now that they were meeting regularly and had clarified their decisions about their goals and operations.

Rachel and Carl's experience is a vivid example of why open, ongoing communication is vital, and that you must not assume you know everything about your partner, even if you've known the person for a long time. Rachel and Carl had been friends for five years and business partners for three, and still conflict arose. Like Rachel and Carl, partners must communicate on a regular basis. All partnerships should have a strategy meeting at least once a week with a quick morning check-in every day to ensure that everyone is on the same page. For Rachel and Carl, additional meetings were necessary for a period of time to address decisions that would become their operational and formal partnership agreements.

ESSENTIAL QUESTIONS: *The two C's that kept Rachel and Carl's partnership afloat are Commitment and Communication. How did transparency and responsibility fit into the picture? Can you see yourself in the original complaint scenario? What would have been your solution if you were Rachel? Carl?*

Ten Reasons Why Partners Don't Use a Written Agreement When They Should

- It never occurs to them that they should.
- They don't know how to write it.
- They think it's an insult to ask someone to put it in writing.
- They think it indicates a lack of trust.
- They think they need a lawyer to do it (they don't) and don't want to pay.
- They think their business arrangement is too small and time limited.
- They don't think their small, short-term arrangement is actually a business.
- They assume that everything is obvious and that they are both/all on the same page.
- One or more has a hidden agenda.
- They plan to do it someday, but never get to it.

And now . . . here's why all the above reasons are not valid:

- People assume that they have heard and understood the other, but often do not. "That's not what I meant."
- People assume that the other person heard and understood them, but they often don't.
- People forget exactly what the other person said. "That's not what I said."
- People forget exactly what they themselves said.
- Misunderstandings, lack of clarity, memory lapses, taking things for granted, making assumptions, not finalizing decisions, having hidden agendas.

Mission and Vision Statements: An Important Part of the BPAT

The mission statement and vision statement that you and your partner(s) agree upon and write into the BPAT will guide you to stay on course in the short and long term. You should also take into account your personal vision statements and, most importantly, your non-negotiable core values. If you and your partner(s) have significant differences in these critical areas, resolve them before you enter the partnership.

In order for a business to have a successful vision and mission, these must be reflected in all aspects of the structure, culture and strategies by which the business is conducted. Together they will be a major part of marketing your brand.

Vision Statement

The vision statement is the big picture of the future you intend to achieve. It is the goal that you have set for yourself and is what you need to think about at all times. It should be the first thing you think about when you begin your work day, and the last thing you think about before you go to sleep. All progress should be measured against your vision. It should be inspiring and inform why you are doing what you do. It may include a time period or not. Your vision is a statement about the future and what you intend to accomplish or become—and this includes each partner's personal vision, as well. What I mean by personal vision is how your personal life goals will fit into the long term of the business.

Remember Bob and Bill, the two brothers? Their personal visions conflicted. One of them wanted to build the business and sell it; the other wanted to hand it down to his children. Each individual partner's personal life vision should also be in sync with the vision of the business in order to ensure that all parties are aligned for the long term in their thoughts and actions. In the case of Bill and Bob, finding out their differing personal goals in advance allowed them to plan for it. If it had come as a surprise, a crisis might have ensued. It's also likely that long-term personal visions may change and therefore cannot be known at the outset. This is what happened when Justin and Romero ended their partnership because of differences in their personal visions. Here's their story:

Partnership is Successful All the Way Through to Exit

Justin and Romero were partners in a chain of do-it-yourself stores for about 15 years. Their shared vision was to build a successful chain of do-it-yourself stores throughout the western United States and have a thriving business to sustain their families for generations. Their mission was to provide easy access to low-cost supplies in various locales for homeowners working on home fix-it projects. The business was successful and throughout the years the two men added a significant number of stores to their chain. While there was a 20-year age difference between the partners, this difference had served them well. Justin was younger and more of a risk taker, Romero older and more cautious. They respected each other's opinions and were able to create a balance in their decision-making. Discussions about investments of profits, adding new stores, dealing with suppliers, and changing their inventory based on changing markets over the years were easy for them. Their partnership was a success.

In year 15, Justin decided it was time to take some new risks by adding additional services like a food and household supply division and a pharmacy. Justin was interested in expanding to include a much broader base of customers; the new additions would not only change the focus of their clientele but also their vendors and marketing strategy. This new vision meant taking risks previously avoided. Justin was eager to move into this new level of business, but at the same time, Romero was thinking of retirement, becoming more cautious and uninterested in forging ahead with such an untested new plan.

Obviously, the changing perspective of the partners' personal goals created a difference of opinion regarding their previous purpose and vision for the business. Communication between the partners had always been open and respectful, so in this situation, the goal of implementing their win/win resolution in the form of their previously carefully crafted exit strategy was simple. The result was a buy-out of Romero's share. The relationship, which had held them in good stead over the years as partners, saw them through to the win/win ending.

ESSENTIAL QUESTIONS: *While you should plan for your most desirable exit outcome, are you also being mindful of the fact that it may not happen that way, but at least you have a place to begin the discussion? Should your main plan not work out for whatever reason, have you discussed plans for every possibility you can envision and created procedures for those outcomes, as well?*

Mission Statement

Like the vision statement, your mission statement defines the measures and standards by which you make all decisions. Contained in the mission statement are the core values and principles set forth by the owners. It answers questions about what you do now, for whom, how and why. It keeps you on track when you ask: is this project, service, employee job description or client in sync with our mission? Doing a checkup like this will always keep you from taking a turn or direction away from your purpose. It will assure your focus. Keep it handy to check all decisions and actions, making sure you are not veering away from your company culture and goals. Team members and employees should have copies of the mission statement for the same reasons.

In the case of the founders of California Pizza Kitchen, Larry Flax and Rick Rosenfield (whom I spoke about earlier) had a mission statement that set a precedent across the entire country. They created what they called a corporate culture, but it's a true mission statement that has been so effective that other companies have adopted it. They call it ROCK: R for respect, O for opportunity, C for communication and K for kindness. With one small business decision, CPK set a precedent that had a monumental effect on changing the country.

In those days (this was back in 1991), restaurants had smoking and non-smoking sections. At a meeting, a manager asked Flax and Rosenfield how under "K for kindness" they could ask a server to work in a smoking section. They immediately agreed and told all the managers to call their restaurants and tell them that they no longer allowed smoking in the restaurants. With that decision, CPK became the first national restaurant chain to ban smoking.

ESSENTIAL QUESTIONS: *Is your business in sync with your mission statement? Do you use it to keep you on track?*

Live Your Mission Today and Plan Your Vision for the Long-Term

Chuck Marquardt and John Barrentine of Red Real Estate Group (whom you also met in an earlier chapter) use their mission statement and core values to monitor and drive everything they do. They discuss it at staff meetings and include it in their marketing. Their mission is to take care of clients at the highest possible level in order to achieve the client's goals. They treat their employees with equal care. Because they value calmness and a well-run life, their vision for the future is to build their team to the point where both can step away and allow the business to operate without them needing to be present. They have practices and procedures in place that minimize chaos. They try to ensure that everything they do is in sync with their mission and long-term vision.

Other Important Elements of the BPAT

Here are some of the other things that the BPAT will present an opportunity for you and your business partner(s) to discuss and decide about:
– Type of business entity
– Equity ownership
– Operations management: what is needed by the business and who is responsible for each area?
– How conflicts will be resolved
– Intentions regarding hiring family
– Schedule of regular meetings and the purpose of each
– Exit strategy for a variety of circumstances

If you believe that thinking through all of these details might not seem necessary at the outset, I offer you the following story about a partnership that ended up in a costly legal battle over one "small" detail: who had the rights to the business name. While I was waiting to be called into the courtroom when on jury duty last year, I sat with a woman who told me about a jury trial she had been on two years earlier. It was a case about a business partnership that had split. It took a jury a week to decide which of the partners could use the name of their now-ended pizza restaurant, *Mama mia!* When you consider that the partners had to spend time preparing their case, going to the hearing, paying their attorneys to battle in court for a week (as well as the cost of tying up the court and jury for five days)—all to make a decision that probably could have been decided in 10 minutes or less at the outset, it seems silly not to take the time to prepare an agreement.

ESSENTIAL QUESTIONS: *Imagine yourself as either one of these partners. How would it have been different for you? What have you been putting off doing that might have a catastrophic or a negative effect on your business or personal life because you haven't done it?*

***

One more story before we move on. You may have read about this one in the business news a few years ago. It involved Joel Meyerson of Miami, Florida, a businessman who invented an anti-aging cream called Strixaderm. In 2004, he and his company, Pure Source, were sued for trademark infringement by Klein Becker, manufacturers of a competing product named Strivectin. Meyerson agreed to the terms of a restraining order, which required him to reformulate, re-market and repackage his product.

In order to do this, Meyerson partnered that same year with Robert Bell, who created the popular Banana Boat suntan lotion brand, which he later sold for $60 million. Bell had also reconstituted Sea & Ski, another successful tanning lotion. Their ownership agreement called for Bell to become a one-third partner in Strixa-derm; Meyerson held a two-thirds stake. A new company, Pure Products, was formed as the new product line's worldwide distributor.

Problems began to arise when Meyerson wanted to move forward quickly and introduce the products to mass-market stores, while Bell wanted to build the brand slowly and methodically. Meyerson wrote Bell to end his contract then several lawsuits ensued. Ultimately, Bell's Beauty Development filed suit against Meyerson, alleging that he siphoned off all the sales and took $520,000 in profits without sharing it with Bell. Bell also alleged that a buyout provision in the contract called for Meyerson to pay Bell $1.8 million. Meyerson countersued for breach of contract and claimed that he had not read the partnership agreement carefully. After mediation failed, both agreed to a bench trial.

The plaintiff (Bell) argued that the fact that Meyerson had not carefully read the partnership agreement carefully was no excuse. A forensic accountant was called as a witness to testify about the profits that should have gone to the distributor and calculate the amount due to Bell under the buyout agreement. The defense (Meyerson) claimed that Bell did none of the work and made zero sales; and since Meyerson did all the work, he deserved the profits. The outcome? The judge awarded $2.49 million in damages to Bell.

This case study illustrates the very important point that a partnership agreement (or my BPAT)—as well as anything else that is created for the business—needs to be the result of conversations and decisions jointly made by the partners to build, define and solidify their partnership. Whether equity is split evenly or not doesn't matter. Any split that creates a partnership is a partnership, and everything that I've written on these pages still applies. As such, there can never be a legitimate scenario in which a partner (like Meyerson) can say, "I didn't read the partnership agreement." Every partner needs to be involved in writing the agreement; and if that is not how it's being done, then expect problems. The good news is that you are learning in these chapters precisely how to avoid such problems every step of the way—from startup through to exit, which is the subject of the next chapter.

Chapter 7
'Til Death or Design Do We Part: Planning a Winning Exit Strategy

> "It's okay to spend a lot of time arguing about which route to take to San Francisco when everyone wants to end up there, but a lot of time gets *wasted in such arguments if one person wants to go to San Francisco and another secretly wants to go to San Diego.*"
>
> –Steve Jobs, cofounder of Apple, Inc.

In *Entrepreneur Magazine*, Dallas Mavericks owner and charismatic entrepreneur Mark Cuban lists his "12 rules for startups." Cuban's Rule #1 is: don't start a company unless it's an obsession and something you love. Yes, yes! I wholeheartedly agree. This is the basis for any successful business. Rule #2 is where I stand my ground to respectfully disagree. Cuban says: if you have an exit strategy, it's not an obsession. No, no! I wholeheartedly disagree! Here's why: Cuban's viewpoint about an exit strategy is based on the belief that it's having one foot out the door.

The better approach, I believe, is to reaffirm the strength of the partnership in every way, knowing that eventually, if not sooner, an exit will occur. For this reason, having an exit strategy from the very beginning—and writing it directly into the BPAT near day one—is another business partnership essential. It is understandable that this is the last thing you may want to consider when just starting out. Why is it needed? Well, because "life happens" and being prepared with a contingency plan is better than being blindsided.

Ideally, an exit strategy should be crafted within the context of your mutual love and obsession for the business (Cuban Rule #1). It should be written to enhance the relationship between partners throughout the life of the business, including the exit. I advocate that its goal is protection and assurance that the business can continue to prosper even when the unmentionable occurs.

Consider this story: I was coaching clients through the "choosing the right partner" stage and they were moving along beautifully on all levels of creating the business and firming up their relationship as partners. Then something unexpected happened. One of them was in a very serious auto accident. The injured partner was going to be debilitated for at least a year and, as a result, both the business and partnership fell apart. There were financial obligations at that point that fell to the remaining partner and the business came to a screeching halt. Thankfully, this situation is unusual but the lesson here is that many things can happen when least expected. I sincerely urge you to step up and create a win/win exit strategy.

DOI 10.1515/9781547400188-007

TIP: An exit strategy should be planned well in advance and should cover all possible bases that can be imagined. Having a buy-sell agreement in place is a good start.

Exit Strategy Considerations

Here are some things to consider when planning an exit strategy:

- Do not wait until a partner is under financial pressure, has unexpected family circumstances, becomes temporarily disabled or has other health issues or even loses interest in order to figure out what to do about it.
- Is one partner hoping to retire sooner than the other partner?
- In the event of the death of a partner, divorce or incapacity, do you want that space filled by their spouse or children? Maybe you do, but possibly you don't.
- What kind of compensation will occur in these events?
- How do your state laws play into your preferences?
- What happens when one of the partners loses interest in the business or becomes burned out? What are each of your requirements for allowing this partner's departure with no harm to the business?
- What will you do in the event of an unsolicited buyout?

Think through and decide on these matters long before the need for a sale or exit occurs. This will minimize the stress and feelings of loss, and it will also serve to maximize the value of your business. Knowing that you have made some decisions at least as a starting point to these tough conversations is valuable information. Bear in mind that decisions you make now (or have made already) can be modified or even completely changed, if necessary. The beauty of having an exit strategy is that it gives everyone peace of mind and frees you up to focus on Cuban's Rule #1: your obsession and love for the business, enhanced by mutual trust and respect.

Enjoying Retirement: Life After the Sale of a Business

Virginia and Marshall are married with grown children. They had shared the running of their lighting business for 20 years and Marshall wanted to sell. Virginia did not and the results were disastrous. They got as far as filing for divorce, but didn't go through with it. Even though they made the decision to stay together, their divergent goals created constant strife between the two of them, which spilled over into the lives of their children. At work, there was constant tension. Employees felt insecure about their jobs and took sides without even knowing the issue.

In our coaching sessions, Virginia was able to express her fears about selling the business. Not having an ongoing income and perhaps not having anything to do with her time—since all she had known for 20 years was going to their place of business—her fears took over her willingness to even consider the sale. For the first time, Marshall gleaned some understanding of her position and took heed. I suggested that they consult with their financial advisor to assess what would be needed to carry them through years of retirement. He was able to create a plan based on other investments they had that, together with the sale, would offer the security they needed.

Finding something to do was a bigger challenge for Virginia, since she hadn't developed a network of friends or a particular interest outside of work. Marshall, on the other hand, planned on taking classes on the many topics that he only mildly had time to dabble in; he felt that his hours would be full and satisfying.

With the financial plan in place, the emotions, tension and arguments lightened. The new, more pleasant atmosphere around the office baffled the employees, but now they were able to focus more on getting things done. I had three more sessions alone with Virginia, at first urging her to take scheduled time away from work and to review catalogs and books to find things that piqued her interest. I also suggested that she find a cause to support and volunteer some of her time. She visited the local museums and fell in love with art. She decided to become a docent at one of them. It took about four months until they found the right buyer. Now, both Virginia and Marshall are enjoying their retirement.

Even married couples should have a long-term vision and an idea of where they would like to land. The discussion should include the notion that the day will come when they no longer want to work. It also should address the "what ifs," like if something happens to one of them, a buyout offer appears, or only one of them wants to continue.

Where children are involved in the picture, succession plans also need to be on the table. In Virginia and Marshall's case, none of their children had an interest in the business. However, at the outset they wouldn't have known that, since the children were young. There may have also been a situation where only one or two of the three would have wanted to inherit it. Discussions around these possibilities could have occurred early on, but certainly at this time they would be a must.

ESSENTIAL QUESTIONS: *Did you notice that compromise became possible when listening was focused on hearing Virginia's reason for not wanting to sell? Can you step back from a disagreement or argument that is ongoing in your life and dig deeper to find out what is behind the stance of the other person? What about your own reasons? Are you each willing to listen to each other and possibly change your mind? Address that level of understanding and you'll get somewhere.*

Your business is not separate from your life. In fact, it is probably the biggest part of your life in terms of time spent. This is why I have made the point that your personal vision has to fit with the vision of the business. They don't have to be the same, just workable.

When leaving a business for any reason, you are smart to have a "go to" plan. What do you do the day after you stop going to this business? Do you want to think in terms of making a different kind of contribution to the world by developing a creative talent? Or volunteer your time to a worthy cause? Perhaps you want to travel, read more or move to a different city, or a different country. Whatever your plan, it is wise to have a plan in place to give you guidance as to what comes next. You may not know exactly what you want to do after your business ends and that's okay. But giving it consideration ahead of time will make the transition away from your business to your next endeavor easier. If you have a spouse, you will likely be having these discussions together.

Planning a winning exit strategy will aid you in envisioning your business when you are ready to leave it. In the earliest stages of creating a partnership, you may or may not know much about your feelings around this, but preliminary discussions noting your aspirations, dreams, visions and thoughts are important. Of course, your plans may be derailed by unexpected life events, so you'll want to revisit your exit strategies at your annual meeting to review, modify and change them as the business progresses.

Do Periodic Assessments of Your Exit Strategy

In considering your exit strategy, you might want to have periodic assessments made by a specialist to value your business. Knowing whether or not your business is doing better this year than last and finding out why can help you use that information as a basis for further growth. If your business is losing money, clients, resources or has high employee turnover, you need to assess why it's happening so you can rectify the situation. Ultimately, if the business is to be sold, whether to a partner who wants out, or to an outside entity, it is wise to know these details in order to move forward and determine a fair price. I've found that far too many small business owners don't know enough about their company's worth.

For example, what if one of the partners becomes critically ill or dies? What happens to his/her part of the business? Consider, in addition, the effect that the business will have on that partner's family. Will the family receive a percentage of the partner's investment in the business? If so, how will you go about distributing those proceeds? What if you have no liquidity at the time? What if one partner wants to sell and take early retirement? Perhaps he or she has lost the passion for the business or simply is ready to move onto something new. How will the business be dissolved and/or dispersed? What if the other partner cannot buy out the retiree or doesn't desire to do so? Can the partnership be sold to someone else? If so, how will the proceeds be divided?

This is where consulting with an expert in other fields, such as law and insurance, is prudent. Did your lawyer write a buy-sell agreement into your partnership agreement? Have you spoken to an insurance agent about key man life and disability insurance or other options?

ESSENTIAL QUESTIONS: *Did you plan for your most desirable exit outcome, mindful of the fact that it may not happen that way? At least you have a place to begin the discussion. Should your main plan not work out for whatever reason, discuss plans for every possibility you can envision and create procedures for those outcomes, as well.*

***

Now let's move ahead to the second essential document that I suggest writing up for your partnership: the partnership agreement.

Chapter 8
The Partnership Agreement: Putting Your Handshake on Paper

"All you need is a plan, a road map, and the courage to press on to your destination."
–Earl Nightingale,
the "Dean of Personal Development,"
Nightingale-Conant

What is the main difference between the BPAT and a lawyer-written partnership agreement? Said in a nutshell, attorneys write for breakup.

When a lawyer writes a partnership agreement, each of you will be advised to have your own lawyer look it over. This sets up an adversarial atmosphere, the same as pre-nuptials do for a marriage—which is the equivalent of talking about divorce when you're intending a peaceful, enduring partnership. This is why I advocate writing the BPAT first to solidify the relationship, then with the information you've just put into it, move onto drafting a partnership agreement.

"The best chance for success with a business partner is to lay a strong foundation for the relationship first using the BPAT," says attorney Liat Cohen of Alperstein, Simon, Farkas, Gillin & Scott, LLP in Encino, California. Liat and I jointly present workshops to business owners on why both the BPAT and a legal partnership agreement are necessary. "After you've completed this template, take that content to a lawyer to draft the legal document. That agreement should include, at the very least, the type of business entity being formed, percentage of interest of each partner, job titles, duties, obligations, investments—monetary or in kind—and sections on how to handle disputes, the sale of the business, its liquidation and/or the death of one of the partners. Once a strong foundation is laid, the partnership can proceed to building a successful business."

For many people entering into a business or joint venture partnership, the only agreement they have between them is a handshake, good intentions and firm belief that they understand and agree with each other. Unfortunately, stopping there is not a great idea. It's not necessarily a matter of lack of trust, but rather coming to a clear understanding in written form. As humans, we're fallible. We sometimes forget, misinterpret or mean different things even when using the same words. We can get overzealous about creating a business and brainstorming about the future of our venture, thereby not considering what might happen to the partnership relationship in the future and how it will impact the business and even your personal lives.

DOI 10.1515/9781547400188-008

A partnership agreement allows you to structure your relationship with your partner(s) for the long haul. You can establish management and financial responsibilities for each of you, what will happen in the event that someone leaves the business, and many other crucial issues. While I hope you never have to take the agreement to court, the BPAT and partnership agreement are great tools to use for reference as you live your business, from beginning to exit.

TIP: No matter how tempting it is, avoid using a free downloadable boilerplate partnership agreement from the Internet. Very often, they are copied templates from other sites, and they leave out important elements and often have mistakes in them. They are not uniquely about you.

Five Key Elements of a Partnership Agreement

Here's a close look at five key elements needed for an effective partnership agreement (based on the decisions you have made in the BPAT) and why they're critical to your success.

1. Financial and Other Contributions by the Partners

This section should include the amount of equity invested by each partner, how profits and losses will be shared, and the pay and compensation for each partner. Are stock shares part of the picture? Will they be part of employee compensation or bonuses? It's critical that you and your partner work out and record who is going to contribute cash, assets and/or professional services to the business before you open your doors to clients. Outline each of these elements very specifically, as later disagreements over contributions and compensation have doomed many promising businesses. Carry the conversation further (you may have done this for writing the BPAT) to include your personal financial obligations, your tolerance for risk and how you made financial decisions in previous businesses. What worked and what didn't?

2. Equity Shares in a Business Partnership

Equity positions can be one of the most difficult elements in setting up a partnership or adjusting it when changes occur in ownership or function. It is common for partners, especially potential partners or those in a startup phase, to feel proprietary about their contributions. How do you measure a product or service created by one partner? How would you measure the value of the partner who founded the business and ran it for a period of time before the second one arrived? Can a valid comparison be made between the respective value of the chef and the operations manager in their restaurant? Is sales and marketing worth more than product design? Can the scriptwriter and the producer of a play be considered of equal value to the partnership? What about the designer of the technology as opposed to the investor?

Financial contributions are the easiest to value because they are inherently measurable. Nonprofit organizations put value on both volunteering time as well as financial contributions. Often the volunteer is valued more than the money, but the money is necessary for the organization to exist. Think of Big Brothers. What good is the money alone if the volunteers are not available to donate their time and be there for the children? Which has the greater value?

Even with the most sophisticated measuring devices, it is difficult to assign truly objective values to these contributions. Moreover, the measures themselves have an element of subjectivity. The problem is that decisions must be made by people whose attitudes, values and personalities differ. One way to help make the decision about equity sharing is for each partner to place a value on his or her own contributions and then value each other's. There will most likely be discrepancies but once on the table, these can be discussed and hopefully resolved at the time of business formation. A delay may undermine both the partnership relationship and the level of success of the business itself. This discussion might be aided by the presence of a coach facilitator.

Let's take the example of Linda and Ryan, who decided to split their equity 50/50 without checking in to see who was actually doing more work at any given time in the business. Even a 50/50 split can have inherent unspoken pitfalls if it is accepted as a matter of course without taking the time and effort to have open, honest discussions upfront. Too often, no matter what split is agreed upon, individual feelings are not expressed or addressed. In the case of Linda and Ryan and others like them—who sit next to each other and not on opposite sides at the conference table—the 50/50 is based on the idea that each will do what the business needs when it needs it. They acknowledge that there are times when one will be expending greater efforts than the other, but both accept the concept that in the long run it all evens out.

No matter what the decided upon equity positions are, the partners are wise to practice ongoing, honest communication, trust in each other and ultimately be committed to the partnership relationship as much as they are to the success of the business. If you've read carefully the stories I've presented so far about successful partnerships, you may have noticed that they do not compare themselves to each other in regard to who is doing what. Each has their areas of responsibility and sometimes one works longer hours or takes on a more difficult task than the other. You may also notice that comparing tasks is like comparing apples and oranges. It's a waste of time, energy and emotions. Dedication, trust, respect for your partner(s)' skills, work ethic and concern for their wellbeing should be your focus.

ESSENTIAL QUESTIONS: *How do you feel about doing more than your partner because your skills may be more needed at a given time? Would you still be willing to have a 50/50 equity split? If not, what would you prefer? Do you think that is the best decision given the business needs and the relationship with your partner? It may be.*

3. Restrictions of Authority and Expenditures

Without an agreement that outlines the authority of each partner, any partner can bind the partnership. For example, one partner might sign a contract with a vendor, incurring a debt for new equipment and could do so without the consent of the other partner--unless this is concretely spelled out in your plan.

Create a plan for the specific ways in which decisions about expenditures will be made and how they will be authorized.

Allison and Stanley are both avid collectors of contemporary art. They had been friends for many years and decided to open a gallery together. Allison and Stanley made choices together as to which artists they would display based on their mutual tastes. They shared the vision of giving opportunities to promising new artists who had made some inroads but needed a boost by having an established gallery selling their work.

Allison was in charge of curating and interacting with visitors and potential clients. Stanley was in charge of the finances. He was better at numbers and Allison was happy to let him run with it. They got into the habit of not discussing expenses and Stanley made decisions based on his own opinion. Basic gallery expenses included not only rent and utilities but insurance, shipping costs, manpower to install the art for each show, printing slick brochures/postcards, reception food and wine, permits, wall labeling, assistants, computers, phone lines, promotional material for the gallery, print ads and sometimes travel to discover emerging artists.

The problem stemmed from Stanley's expensive tastes. He loved to plan expensive receptions that were too high-end for the budget: fine wine instead of Trader Joe's, and food by famous chefs in the area instead of a more reasonably priced catering company. He often let artists off the hook for paying for shipping costs. The day finally arrived when he had to tell Allison that they were close to bankruptcy. They decided to cut their losses, work out payment plans with creditors and close the gallery.

Often partners think all they need to do is work in their areas of expertise and responsibility and let the other partners do the same. When done this way, no one is monitoring the big picture and each one is taking a pass on being responsible for the business as a whole.

ESSENTIAL QUESTIONS: *What could have prevented the bankruptcy and closure of this business? By now you know there were many times in the process when things could have been done differently.*

4. Partner Duties and Responsibilities

This is where you outline duties in advance of opening your doors. Who is in charge of accounting? Product design? Who is the technology guru? Who is handling hiring employees and negotiating salaries? Who is overseeing vendor management? Who will be making purchases and writing the checks? Who is in charge of sales and marketing, and bringing in new customers? Go through your day-to-day operational needs and make sure that your plan covers everything that the business needs, not just the areas you as partners divide up. Discuss these along with each other's strengths and weaknesses when delineating authority so that each partner's skills are utilized to the best possible ability. These should have already been outlined in the BPAT, and now simply transcribed into the partnership agreement.

Gregory and James were co-founders of a startup software development company, and their story is an unfortunate example of what can happen when tasks are not delineated. Both of them were technology experts, but James knew more about it than Gregory. Based on that, they decided that James would be in charge of technology and software development, support of the company websites, and all information systems. Gregory would be in charge of marketing, advertising and PR related projects, as well as finances and finding new investors. In order to get the business up and running, Gregory put up an initial $75,000 and James, who had less, added $25,000. They didn't spell out anything specific about the partnership, equity split or matters regarding finances. Because each had very distinctive and different tasks, they didn't feel the need to meet and discuss the business, nor had they bothered to write any kind of partnership agreement. They just assumed their own tasks and worked by themselves.

Unfortunately, after 10 months, Gregory began to feel that James was not pulling his weight. Yet James was sure that he was putting in much more time than Gregory. James called me to save them. We had four sessions but the goal was to part amicably and fairly, since Gregory no longer wanted to continue in the business. Because of their lack of communication, it felt like each had gone their separate ways. They didn't even have a proper accounting of the business's worth at that point. James valued his product development differently than Gregory, who saw himself as the majority partner because of the larger sum of money he had invested.

James was the one who called me for help. It was a difficult resolution and I made them each aware that the outcome would likely not be the one that either of them preferred. As I do in these situations, I sent them each away for three days with a homework assignment: do not speak to each other for three days, write two plans that would be acceptable as a solution to you and write a solution from the viewpoint of the other person (in other words, what you think your partner would want as a solution).

When they returned, Gregory and James had learned a lot about themselves and each other. After presenting the three plans they each had written, I helped them choose a version that they ultimately could compromise on and accept. Neither got what he wanted, but they did gain a new level of understanding about themselves and each other. In that sense, it was a win for both and a painful lesson about choosing the right partner and properly setting up a business.

ESSENTIAL QUESTIONS: *By now you can identify the mistakes they made. How should they have done it differently? What would you have done as Gregory? As James?*

5. Dispute Settlement Strategy

It is helpful and essential to have a plan to resolve disagreements and stalemates among partners. You may have an equity split of 50/50, 60/40 or any other ratio. Regarding the arena of conflict resolution, some partners use a 49/51 split based on a partner's area of expertise. This means that the person with, for example, expertise in design takes the extra point to make the final decision about design. When there is a disagreement or stalemate pertaining to technology, the partner with the expertise has the 51st share and makes the final decision to upgrade their telecommunication system. Another option would be to call in a third-party expert in that field (not one who sells the product), or a coach or mediator. A third option might be as simple as flipping a coin. Make sure that you choose whichever option feels most right for you and your partner then write it into both the BPAT and partnership agreement. You can always change this option, but having something in place ahead of any dispute will ensure that no one has to worry in the heat of the moment about what to do to resolve the stalemate. Again, if you've been in a partnership for a while but still have not written a partnership agreement, it's never too late to do so, as the following case study proves.

Even college buddies can benefit from having a partnership agreement, as Marge and Lori's situation illustrates. The two had been friends since studying design at their university. Marge started a business designing and manufacturing uniforms for professional chefs. About a year later, she and Lori decided to partner in the business. They worked well together. Their skills were not complementary, as partners usually look for in each other. They pretty much had the same skills. The two of them planned the designs, and created and marketed their products successfully as a result of collaborating every day about everything. Their business was growing and the women knew they'd eventually need to add personnel, but for the time being, the two of them did everything and enjoyed it.

Still, they had one issue that threatened their relationship. When they talked about it and tried to resolve it on their own, they always argued. They were smart enough to see the threat it posed not only to the business but their friendship. That's when they called me. The issue was that Marge felt she should be compensated for the time she started the business and Lori hadn't yet come into it. Lori refused to acknowledge any validity in Marge's claim.

On one hand, when they talked about the business, I could hear the joy and satisfaction they each derived from it and the way they worked in sync. On the other hand, the tension was palpable when they called me to help. As always, the first thing I did was help them listen to each other as if they were the other person. This always lowers the volume of emotion and the partners can be more rational in their willingness to compromise.

I asked each of them to write two solutions that they would be willing to accept while taking into account the other person's position; I required that they do this exercise without talking to each other about this issue until our next session. Lori's willingness to acknowledge the extra time and money invested by Marge gave Marge a level of satisfaction in and of itself. Lori had worried that Marge would be asking for endless financial compensation, which she now saw was not the case. Marge was happy to settle for additional vacation time in that year and then close the subject forever. In two coaching sessions, it was resolved. They hadn't written a partnership agreement previously, so they took my advice and completed the BPAT. We had one more coaching session to help clarify some of the issues they needed help with, and since then their business has grown for four years and they now have nine employees.

ESSENTIAL QUESTIONS: *How differently would you have handled this issue? Do you believe that the business and their friendship would have ended because of this argument if they hadn't called me or someone else to help work it out? Would it have been an issue if you were Marge? What fears about it would you have had, as Lori did? Would you have accepted the settlement that Marge agreed to?*

***

Much of the information that you and your partner(s) have drafted in the BPAT and partnership agreements will now get extra mileage in the business plan, which is the next essential written document that I recommend, for not just partnerships arrangements, but for any professional venture. Let's dive into the business plan now.

Chapter 9
The Future is Now: Formulating Your Business Plan

"Plan for what is difficult while it is easy."

—Sun Tzu, "The Art of War"

It always amazes me how casually so many entrepreneurs jump into business with a partner—or even a solo venture, for that matter—without a solid plan. Chemistry with a prospective partner might get you in bed together, but what happens in the morning? Some believe that having capital is enough. Others think that if they have an idea, complementary skills, or a shared vision, it's enough. Maybe one of them owns an appropriate real estate site for the business, so the partners hop on the bandwagon and start the trip, not seeing the chasm in the road ahead that will totally derail them. These early mistakes, made somewhat impulsively because of the enthusiasm to get started, are some of the reasons for that 70% business partnership failure rate.

Now that you have your agreements in place and have mapped out an exit strategy, putting your business plan on paper is the next absolutely essential endeavor. Don't launch a company without it. (Don't even try!) This document can be drafted as you are working through your BPAT and partnership agreement, but if you haven't prepared it yet, now is the time to do so. Among many other details, it should address things like the feasibility of your business and its physical location. The degree to which you take the time to do an actual feasibility study depends on the complexity, size, mission, location and available finances. As the following story cautions, some minimal assessment should always take place.

Of the two frozen yogurt businesses that opened in my neighborhood a few years ago, one is thriving and the other is gone. The successful one is on a busy street in proximity to fast food chain eateries and clothing stores, FedEx and a large chain grocery store. There is ample street parking and lots of foot traffic from the nearby stores and offices. The one that is gone opened on an equally busy parallel thoroughfare a few blocks away, where there was also plenty of street parking but no foot traffic. The neighborhood is a destination for those who want furniture refinishing and auto repairs. It's not likely that many people would leave their chairs for repair and walk a few yards for yogurt. Many eager business owners overlook important details like this. Never ignore red flags.

DOI 10.1515/9781547400188-009

Your Business Plan is a Living Document

Your business plan should not be a lifeless, lengthy document that you labored to create, only to have it sit in a drawer or on your hard drive. Rather, turn it into an ever-evolving action plan that is unique to your business, a tool that you use as a guide and revise on a regular basis. Since you've moved from dating your business partner to writing the BPAT and partnership agreement, you will already have a good bit of the content of your business plan. It doesn't have to be done all at once; it can be addressed in any order based on the information you currently know. Also, it can evolve from the time you begin your business through every stage of growth. As you compile each section and describe your business, your commitment to it will be that much stronger because you are making decisions in the process. You will be able to see it and sense it while you plan it.

There are different approaches and opinions about business plans that you can easily access on the Internet, as well as various templates. Feel free to use the guide that I provide in this book, choose a different one that works better for you, write your own or create a combination. If you use a boilerplate rendition or any other, including the one I mention here, you will still need to make it your own by adding sections and content that describe the uniqueness of your business and specific industry. Note that if your business is a spa, a tech firm, a medical group, gym, clothing shop, furniture designer, hardware store, children's toy company, a bed and breakfast, landscaper, food service provider, financial institution or anything else, the way you answer these questions will vary greatly. Don't settle for the vagueness that will emerge by using someone else's template even if your industry is the same or similar. You will want your plan to be very specific. One exception regarding the use of a template is if you are going to seek investors; in that case, you will have to comply with the one they provide.

The template I am offering here is a basic working document that you can change, add to and certainly reevaluate periodically. Change it in any way that will make it better suited to your needs and industry specificities. Remember, this is a fluid document. If you don't have all the information required now, begin writing anyway.

A Typical Business Plan Outline

Executive Summary

- Co-owners' names and addresses.
- History of the firm and how the partner(s) came together.
- Name of business and location.
- Define your mission and vision statements.
- Describe the products and/or service you are offering.
- Who is your target market?
- Describe your competition.
- How is your business different from others that are similar?
- What are your general financial goals? (Get more detailed in the financial plan section.)
- Brief statement about how capital needs will be met, with more details in the financial plan section.

Business Strategy

- How does your business differ from competitors? What is your competitive edge?
- What feasibility studies have you done? How do you know the market will buy?
- Include figures and graphics that demonstrate your claims based on research of this market.
- Discuss the processes you will use, such as online technology.

Financial Plan

- What are your current startup or expansion capital needs?
- What resources do you have for these finances?
- What is each partner contributing financially, in kind, or with intellectual property or time?
- What are your assets and liabilities now?
- What are your staff requirements now and for the next three to five years?
- Describe duties that the staff will perform.

– Describe your projected income, expenses and cash flow information for each period up through five years.

Marketing Strategy

– What is your marketing budget?
– Describe your market and sales goal for year one and growth projections for the first five years.
– What are your marketing and sales strategies?
– Describe your plan and costs for pricing, advertising, promotions and forecasts for each progressive year.
– Who will be your marketing personnel? Who will be your sales personnel?
– Who will manage these departments?

Community Participation

– Will your business be adopting or supporting a specific cause or non-profit organization?
– Is giving back part of your value system and is it spelled out in your mission statement?

Areas of Responsibilities and Tasks

– Discuss and write the details of what each partner will be responsible for. This is extremely important.
– List all tasks not covered by one of you and decide on the number of employees required and the skills, expertise and responsibilities that should be assigned to them.
– After doing the above, day-to-day and long term tasks can be assigned effectively. Delegating is an art. It takes practice. (See more tips about delegating in Additional Resources at the end of the book.)

★★★

As I've pointed out already, many relationships get into trouble when partners blame each other for doing less than they initially said they would. Others suffer due to partners overstepping their bounds or authority. Clearly written areas of responsibility in your plan will act as a reference and checkpoint to prevent such instances from happening. One of the partners may actually do the tasks in a particular area or there may be employees who are delegated to do it.

No matter what, all partners are responsible to know what is happening, not in a micro-managing sense, but as it relates to the company's goals and purpose. I am emphasizing this because it is important: each partner is responsible for the whole business, so when things go wrong in an area assigned to your partner, even if you've used that as a reason not to pay attention, you are also 100% responsible.

Make sure that your business plan is concise, clear, and always up to date. Keep in mind that it is apt to change over time for a variety of reasons that will become apparent as time goes on. Make sure that its format is easily accessible and able to be edited. While time consuming and necessarily thought provoking, you will find that a business plan is extremely worth the time and effort you put into it, as it can go a long way in helping to ensure your business's success.

Chapter 10
Life Happens: Preparing for "What Ifs" and the Unexpected

"It is not the strongest of the species that survive, not the most intelligent, but the ones most responsive to change."

–Charles Darwin

Lee Ann and Bruce owned a highly successful business for many years, designing and manufacturing outdoor furniture. Then something happened that they'd never planned for: the company began to suffer due to a serious downturn in the economy. Still, Lee Ann and Bruce didn't discuss what to do about it; rather, they continued to hold onto the company while simply wishing away any misfortune.

After a few years of struggling to stay afloat, Lee Ann decided that the solution was to sell. Bruce was nowhere ready to do this. They had endless discussions, which culminated in a few adjustments. They moved into smaller quarters, adapted their product line, found more cost-effective vendors and let go of most of their employees. Basically, the plan was to ride out the economic hardship and find their way up again soon.

These measures were not enough and the business didn't improve; in fact, the downturn continued. Both became tense and stressed, which translated into arguments and disagreements about what to do. This took an emotional and physical toll on Lee Ann personally and on Bruce's marriage. Finally, Bruce agreed to sell and they listed the business with a broker. Sadly, they were not able to recoup anything close to what they lost.

Bruce and Lee Ann's story brings up several important questions: Could they have prepared for this "what if" scenario in advance? If so, what plan could they have talked about early on that could have spared them the emotional suffering and financial loss?

So, we come to the fourth essential written document that should be prepared at the outset of any business partnership. This document is created to enable business partners to confer on unexpected events, and their mutually agreed upon solutions, so that such conversations do not occur in the midst of a crisis. It can be completed after or at the same time that you are working on the previous three documents. Preparing for the unexpected means you are aware that things happen, but you don't know what, when or why. Since the unexpected is usually a crisis to varying degrees, it is better to have an emergency plan already in place to deal with it.

DOI 10.1515/9781547400188-010

When a crisis hits and emotions are heightened, this is not the time to decide on how to handle sensitive issues. Talk about it in a constructive way and lay the groundwork for dealing with problems in advance. Some of these issues will also be part of the BPAT so you will be covering both at the same time. No matter what stage of a business partnership you are in, you will benefit by doing this. Even if you have been in a business partnership for many years, it offers an opportunity to discuss and plan for the events of life and business that have yet to happen . . . and hopefully won't.

Not all crises will require the same response. Each plan you make will give you a starting place that you may modify in the actual situation as it unfolds. Here are some prompts that you can use for discussion and decision-making.

Vision What Ifs

Once you begin clarifying your company vision, use it to brainstorm any unforeseeable situations, such as:

What if one of you decides that you don't want to expand although you may have agreed to a projected growth plan? Make a plan as to what actions will be taken should one of you decide to be content with what you have, while the other is still very much shooting for the moon.

Finance What Ifs

- What if a third-party investor begins to pursue either of you for an "in" to the business? It can be a great opportunity, especially if the investor is bringing a missing piece to the table. How will you protect your partnership and the investments you've already made?
- What if the business is in the red and one partner wants to make a personal loan? What conditions will be allowed/not allowed in dire times? How will the partnership be protected?
- What if a partner is skimming the account to meet the needs of a personal crisis? Unfortunately, this happens. Make sure you have solid procedures in place that you and your partner both agree on in order to prevent this occurrence from happening or deal with it if it does. You may start by reaffirming that you each can openly talk about your hardships to the other.
- What if your biggest account leaves without warning?

Employee What Ifs

— What if one partner wants to hire a family member and the other is against it?
— What if there is an accusation of sexual harassment?
— What if a partner attempts to date an employee?

Daily What Ifs

— What if one partner is a workaholic and the other is laid back?
— What if a local nonprofit approaches for a donation of time, money or in-kind contribution?

Personal Life What Ifs

— What if an accident or illness prohibits one of the partners from being able to carry out their responsibilities in the business for the long term? For the short term?
— What if one of you gets bored and loses interest in the business?
— What if a spouse gets a position across the country and the family needs to move?
— What if a partner faces a divorce or child custody issues and becomes consumed by the proceedings?
— What if one of you becomes disabled?

Exiting What Ifs

— What if the vision fades or ends? Let's face it: not all ideas are great and not all great ideas are marketable. When is it time to throw in the towel? What are some benchmarks that will help you decide?
— What if a partner walks out with clients and accounts?

In addition to the above, think of other possibilities and talk about them, then write down your decisions. You will be glad you did, just in case any of these "what ifs" ever happen.[1]

---

[1] My handbook, *The What If Scenario Handbook to Prepare for the Unexpected Before it Occurs*, was devised precisely for this purpose, with partnership crisis management in mind. As its name implies, this 56-page e-book walks business partners through conversations that should occur and decisions that should be made before a crisis happens. See the Introduction for more information.

Part III: **After the Honeymoon**

Chapter 11
Finding Your Daily Rhythm

"Each partner needs to acknowledge that no matter who did what or how much, nothing could have been accomplished without the work and contribution of the other."

–Lee H. Igel, assistant professor at
New York University's School of Continuing
and Professional Studies

Once all written documents are in place, the focus going forward turns to finding a good working rhythm to ensure ongoing, meaningful communication among the partners. By now, we've clearly established the importance of choosing the right business partner. In many cases, however, it's not choosing the wrong partner that leads to a breakup, but rather partners not knowing how to build and maintain a successful relationship over time.

Let's face it: Day-to-day and week-to-week life can get hectic and even chaotic. Doing business can become a series of extinguishing fires with no one paying attention to the big picture. Without regular partner communication, you run the risk that the business might spiral out of control without anyone noticing. When this happens, the best-case scenario is that the bottom line loses ground, and the worst case can be tragic loss on various levels.

Biggest Tip in This Book: The most important key to success that all partners must know about from the very beginning and do forever is to keep the conversation going using highly skilled communication tools.

Keeping the Home Fires Burning

A business that runs well and is successful requires an ongoing, never-ending conversation from the outset among the partners. A structure must be in place in order to do this. It does not mean, for example, that you have similar work styles, but it does require talking about any differences and finding solutions to work them out and bridge the gaps.

To this end, meeting regularly is crucial to the success of your partnership; and yet, this is commonly avoided by business partners. Why? Well, as is often the case, not a lot gets accomplished if the meetings are not well run. They are thought of as boring and time consuming; and sometimes, emotions take over when disagreements come up. Still, as a partnership coach, I insist that

DOI 10.1515/9781547400188-011

partners meet (also with their teams) on a regular basis. Partners who do not have ongoing meetings to clarify, plan and strategize are jeopardizing their very partnership and the business. What I know for a fact is that when partners and departments within a business don't talk to each other, at the very least, money is left on the table; and when it gets worse, I get the call to rescue a dying partnership relationship.

Sure, it's easy to get caught up in the daily grind, dealing with issues as they arise and spending your days putting out fires. If that's the case, you are not maximizing potential. Ask yourselves if you use this modus operandi as an excuse to avoid addressing difficult issues. You've read stories here about this type of scenario, as well. Did you see yourselves in them?

When communication becomes rare and routine, automated listening replaces active listening. Even when there's dialogue, understanding may be limited. So, let's talk about the types of meetings to have and how to set the rhythm so that they happen with regularity and are well prepared and productive.

Daily Meetings

You may have noticed that the successful partnerships I've included in this book all touch base daily. Generally, the most effective partnerships do this to check in, prioritize, divide tasks, and discuss new problems needing solutions and who will take the lead in resolving them. Sometimes a personal issue might need to be addressed. In strong partnerships, all partners sincerely regard the wellbeing of each other and each is ready to fill in for the others when needed. Daily meetings are often brief and can be held in person or using available technology, such as video conferencing software.

Weekly Meetings

These meetings need to be tightly run, since they are often time- and agenda-sensitive. It is best if all members are present, as these meetings offer a forum for deeper discussion than the daily meetings. I offer the following scenario as a good example of an efficient outcome of weekly meetings.

One of my clients is a group of partners whose business functioned by having separate divisions that never met together: sales, marketing, design and fulfillment. The partners preferred to "manage" the business mostly by email. Communication became hampered over time and problems began to arise. As I coached this group, they decided to introduce weekly meetings, where all team members could come together to talk about what everyone was doing. The benefits were immediate. Team members saw the value of collaboration, as the business began to function at a higher capacity. The meetings also gave all the team members a sense of the bigger picture and how they as teams and individuals fit into the business. Eventually, the bottom line reflected this smoother rhythm of operation.

Monthly Meetings

It's up to the partners to decide the purpose and who participates in these meetings. It may be partners only, or with managers or with an outside expert, such as lawyer, CPA, coach or someone else pertinent to the discussions that need to take place. Often, the purpose of monthly meetings is to strategize, set goals and evaluate progress made in previous months and plan for the next month, quarter or season. An employee might be invited to attend and should feel safe to express opinions and ask for support, training or whatever that individuals needs to improve his or her job performance.

Annual Meetings

Annual meetings are vital for planning, reviewing and analyzing the business. Holding annual meetings with your management team to discuss where you have been and where you want to go is a sound way to maximize your business operations. One of the main requirements for finding your rhythm is to revisit annually all large decisions you have made. At a minimum, this includes a review of your business plan and BPAT, including how your mission and vision statements are working for you, areas of responsibility, clarity of roles, and what-if decisions. This is the time to evaluate your previous year's accomplishments and set goals for the coming year. This review sets up a framework for the structure and rhythm of your business, just like the seasons of the year add context to our lives. It may take place as an annual retreat away from your offices. It may include reports from managers or other key employees that you've hired over time, or their actual presence for at least part of the discussions.

What Happens Within the Meetings

Maintaining the discipline of this regular rhythm of meetings, each with a purpose, will keep everyone focused on executing the strategic plan and mission on a daily basis. This focus is the key to getting results.

Rhythm is also what happens within the meetings. Discuss what type of rhythm you wish to achieve and how many meetings you think you may need. What is the appropriate length, frequency, number of attendees and, most importantly, the agenda? As all business partnerships are unique, there is no standard for how often you must meet, though I do recommend that you try some configuration—whether it be for daily, weekly, monthly and annual meetings—to zone in on how you can most effectively run your business.

TIP: Set the rhythm by scheduling daily, weekly, monthly, annual and team meetings, then stay accountable for making them happen.

ESSENTIAL QUESTIONS: *Do you meet regularly? If not, why not? Are your agendas clear, easy to get through and productive? Are your meetings respectful and friendly?*

Meeting Topics for Discussion

The following is a list of selected topics for discussion at your regular meetings. Not everything on this list will apply to your business or need to be discussed at every meeting. There may be some things, perhaps industry specific, that are not listed here, so add them to your agenda. Always start each meeting with checking in about anything that is happening at the moment. There could be, for instance, a grievance or annoyance that needs to be resolved before it spirals out of control.
 — Personal issues between you and those in your outside life that affect your business
 — Personal issues between you as partners
 — A new idea
 — Finances and cash flow
 — Operations and staff
 — A particular employee
 — Compliance issues
 — Sales and marketing
 — Equipment or technology

- Products and design
- Employee issues and team building
- Hiring or letting someone go
- Targeting your ideal customers
- Your competitors
- Community relations and philanthropy
- SWOT analysis (a good tool for planning)
- Changes in attitude toward the business (do you all still love it?)
- Dealing with the unexpected scenarios

***

Each of these meeting categories and others is crucial to the overall high functioning of your business, so why would you ignore discussing them? If one of you or someone else on your team is in charge of any of these areas, you as an owner still must know what's going on and be involved in the decision-making at some level.

Changes and modifications are the nature of life's journey, both personally and in business. As a result, nothing you have decided upon in Parts I and II of this book is written in stone. So go ahead and change things up! Decide in advance how frequently you will review your plans, and write this timeline into the operations part of your business plan, BPAT and partnership agreement. Then stick to your commitment to meet regularly and talk through whatever arises in the normal course of running your business. As always, the only non-negotiable item should be your commitment to being open, honest and respectful at all times.

Chapter 12
Listen Up: Essential Communication Skills

"There is no limit to what a man can do or where he can go if he doesn't mind who gets the credit."

—Robert Woodruff

You may already be in a solid partnership, one that's lasted for years. Regardless, I suggest that you take a closer look at how things are going. Very often, partners get into the habit of maintaining a facade that "everything's okay" because things are running along as they always have. Upon closer observation, however, this habit may be a reason for avoiding talks about issues that need to be discussed for the health of the business, but that one or both partners find easier to ignore. Many partnerships last for decades, seemingly successful, and then they erupt, ending painfully and expensively in court, when one partner is shocked to discover hidden animosity or other negative feelings that have been smoldering in the background for some time.

This is why I recommend periodic checkups, at least yearly, as outlined in the previous chapter. Ideally, these periodic checkups should be mediated by an outside consultant. The benefit of having a third-party expert run through some of the ways you function with each other will help you to recognize the blind spots—and, believe me, they are there. It's just human nature that we can't see ourselves objectively. Even great athletes, artists and orators need a coach to point out their weaknesses, as well as their strengths. Speaking of which, coaching can help you to identify ways in which you already deal with the business issues and each other that work well. If you can't see what you are doing wrong, you may also not notice what you are doing right. When you know what you are doing right, even by rote, you can consciously put those methods into your toolbox, build on them and pull them out when things get a little rough. In the process, additional new and even better ways can be created and strategized. There is always room to do it better.

ESSENTIAL QUESTIONS: *Is there something I avoid speaking to my partner about because it feels too painful, annoying, or confrontational? Is there anything my partner is avoiding bringing up for one of those same reasons? How about taking the first step toward having the conversation?*

DOI 10.1515/9781547400188-012

Improve Your Listening Skills

I can't stress enough that the most important tool for successful partnership relationships is communication—which is, for the most part, good listening. This is not the same as listening in order to make your case or get your way, but listening to hear deeply and respect the other's point of view while being open to possibly (but not necessarily) changing yours. Active listening, or paraphrasing what was said to be sure you have understood correctly, shows that you value the connection with your partner(s) and are committed to respecting their opinions. Sometimes this can be a tall order, but you can easily practice and enhance your active listening skills. Here are four suggestions:

Get rid of the idea that you have to be right

You can't learn what you think you already know. If you have an investment in being right, you have already closed down your ability to hear. Besides, if you think you are always right, the other person is always wrong, and this sets up a surefire system for the destruction of communication lines. Such a stance will wreak havoc on your partnership and business

Listen with an open mind

Recognize that there are many ideas and perspectives besides your own. Many of them are good and some may be better than yours

Actively participate by giving positive feedback

As you participate in the conversation, repeat back to your partner what you heard in order to make sure you have clearly understood. Ask questions when things are not clear. An open mind when listening will help you more clearly receive and interpret information.

Allow for the possibility that you have something to learn from the other person

Often people reject an expressed idea when it's different from their own, even though another's viewpoint and ideas may produce more (and better) ideas. Before you know it, a once unwanted idea has expanded your options and created new and exciting possibilities. If, instead, new ideas aren't generated, you can take comfort in the fact that you have respectfully listened to others' opinions and feelings; in doing so, you may have cleared the air about something that was standing in the way of your business moving forward.

Forget about preparing your response

That's right, no pre-work required! Active listening means you are fully engaged. Preparing your response will block you from actually hearing what is being said. Respond only *after* you have listened. There is nothing wrong with taking your time to formulate a response. If you want time to mull something over, say so and promise to get back to your partner about it. Express your own thoughts and feelings honestly and respectfully.

***

Becoming a better listener will benefit not only your business partnership but also the relationships in your personal life. Give yourself something fun to look forward to with these conversations and enjoy the experiences you're gaining from being in a partnership. For example, conduct brainstorming sessions in which all ideas are received without criticism, no matter how absurd they initially sound. Remember that you and your partner(s) are in this together, so don't be afraid to add a dose of humor into these conversations.

Since active listening is a learned discipline, it pays to practice, practice, practice. One way to do so is to create conversations solely for the goal of enhancing these skills. The following is a quick questionnaire to help you refine your active listening skills. It can be difficult to listen without projecting your own motives, so if you find yourself answering these questions in a way that you perceive as wrong, know that these answers do not define you; this is simply information for you to use as you progress in this area.

- When you listen, are you preparing your next reply?
- Do you jump in and interrupt, assuming you know what the other person wants to say?

- Are you listening with the willingness to learn and the possibility of having your mind changed?
- Do you listen with empathy for the other's point of view?
- Do you listen with the intention of finding a win-win solution to the problem or conflict?
- Do you handle disagreements graciously, without being critical of anyone?
- Do you keep meeting discussions confidential? Don't gossip about who said what.

ESSENTIAL QUESTIONS: How do you rate yourself as a communicator? Good skills require practice. Take notice when you are talking with someone and see if you are truly listening based on the questions above.

TIP: Practice "not listening" when you are talking with someone. Next, just stop and actually This is the first step to improving your skills. listen to what is being said.

The Value of Compromise

Compromise is a valuable commodity among partners and is critical to successful partnerships. It entails keeping the big picture in mind and adopting an attitude of "what I get from this partnership is worth my being flexible." When used properly, compromise helps the communication lines remain open and effective. Again, it helps to bear in mind that, as partners, you are a team that merges into one entity with the goal of providing whatever the business needs. On that basis, compromise is attainable, when necessary.

Consider the partnership between Angie and Eric, whose differences in work styles is a frequent area where compromise is necessary. Angie is a designer in their interior design firm. Eric serves as sales manager and is also in charge of inventory and finances. Angie is a "get it done yesterday" person, whose desk is always clean. Eric is a last-minute man; his desk is piled with papers in seeming chaos.

When I met them, there was great tension between them based only in this area. Generally, they got along well, sharing values about how to treat employees, customers and vendors. They were on the same page in every other important way but their good relationship was being eroded by Angie's constant complaining about Eric's work habits. Fortunately, their commitment to resolve this was strong. Eric was willing to hear that Angie's carping about his style was based on her fear that things weren't getting done. He was able to show her that, in fact, everything was done and on time as promised. Every order was fulfilled and collections, salaries, payments to vendors and new orders were being made exactly on time—despite what looked like chaos to Angie. When Eric assured Angie that he understood her fears, she agreed to focus on his end result and ignore his messy desk. The issue was never brought up again.

ESSENTIAL QUESTIONS: *Can you envision such a strong commitment to the business and to the partnership that you would be able to overlook a great difference in work styles? How might this story have ended differently? Do either of these partners remind you of yourself? Your partner?*

Compromise was also the key to rectifying the partnership between Bryan and Tim, co-founders of a shoe manufacturing company. Bryan called me from his office in Baltimore, Maryland, complaining that he was going to walk out if I didn't rescue his partnership. He said that Tim didn't work much and, as a result, Bryan was doing far more than his share. As is my practice, I asked him to get Tim on the phone, as well. We set up an appointment for the three of us, where I asked each of them to tell what was happening in their own words, while the other listened without judging.

This revealed a number of misunderstandings. Each of them had different responsibilities: Bryan was in charge of all financial issues, technology and inventory. Tim was in charge of sales and marketing. As I've mentioned already, when partners have different skills and work assignments, measuring value based on time spent is like comparing apples and oranges, yet each role is indispensable. Often partners with different responsibilities tend to work in their own areas and ignore coming together to talk about the big picture. That is what was happening between Bryan and Tim. Like many other partners, they made excuses around time constraints and in truth were each busy putting out fires—another common, destructive way in which business owners and managers function. As with many partnerships, not meeting regularly was the reason for the distance created between them. As a result, Bryan came to the conclusion that Tim wasn't doing his share and his resentment had built up so much tension that they couldn't talk to each other without my facilitation.

Fortunately, they both were committed to the success of the business and were open to changing their dysfunctional avoidance of each other. They were ready to make some changes. From our first session on, I lowered the volume of tension and emotion between them by allowing each one to share his viewpoint, and making sure each listened carefully to the other and was able to repeat back what he heard. We did this until the speaker was sure his position was clearly heard and understood.

If business partners don't let the bad feelings get beyond repair to the point where they have one foot on the courthouse steps, but instead are committed to making it work, a rescue is possible. What typically happens within one to three sessions is that we get to the point where the partners rediscover that they are not so far apart in their desires, dreams and goals. Using the tools we have discussed, we can restart the relationship and fill in all of the gaps created by the lack of communication and decision-making that were missing from the beginning. Then we are able to use newly acquired communication skills, create a functional infrastructure, and schedule regular meetings that are on target.

That's what I did with Bryan and Tim. With practice, they accepted my suggestion to set up weekly partnership meetings, always with a meaningful agenda, covering the important issues of the week. They embraced the notion that if there was something that bothered either of them about the other, they must bring it up immediately and listen respectfully to the other, then find a resolution that both could accept.

Tim and Bryan were able to see that they were losing a lot of business by not having team meetings with their managers. They discovered that relationships were important throughout the business; in other words, it was crucial that designers, marketers and fulfillment people worked together as a team and welcomed suggestions and ideas from everyone. Aside from the positive effect that it had on the efficiency of the business, doing this also created among the 25 managers and employees the feeling that everyone's opinions were being heard and valued. After operationalizing these forms of ongoing communication in three months, Tim and Bryan both admitted that they were seeing a more robust bottom line.

ESSENTIAL QUESTIONS: *How would you have handled this differently before calling for coaching? What would your thoughts have been about Tim if you were Bryan and vice versa?*

***

Eventually in any partnership, after the courtship and honeymoon end, daily life takes over. As we discover our daily rhythm, we may begin to notice things in our significant other that unnerve or even upset us, and we're not as eager as we once were to gloss over them. Partnerships on the success track will welcome opportunities to speak honestly to resolve whatever challenges bubble up in the course of business. If the partners' commitment to one another and the company is unshakeable, they will want to find an amicable solution.

Yet what happens when differences and disagreements reach a boiling point? How do you gauge whether the problem is just a quickly passing emotional squall or a firestorm that's been raging out of control for some time? Let's go there now.

Chapter 13
Trouble in Paradise? Conflict Resolution Basics

"Problems do not go away. They must be worked through or else they remain forever a barrier to the growth and development of the spirit."

-M. Scott Peck,
*The Road Less Traveled: A New Psychology of
Love, Traditional Values and Spiritual Growth*

I can say this with certainty: there isn't a business partnership out there that isn't in some process of development, maturation or maintenance, and these stages don't occur in a straight line. They overlap and repeat. Co-founders have excellent days and exasperating days. Sales can shoot up, then slow to a crawl. The relationship can show signs of strain and tension, then rebound with renewed vigor and sense of purpose.

When a crisis manifests, it can take many forms. Like a marriage partnership, the friction can build slowly then become a pebble in the shoe, no longer able to be ignored without a little pain. Others can appear overnight: a surreptitious betrayal by one of the partners, or a downturn in business that isn't easily recouped. Some disputes are predictable; others are borderline irrational. At such times, the succeed-or-fail trajectory may go one way or the other. Successful partnerships will recommit to their goals by stepping up their communication to resolve issues. Those doomed to self-destruct will have at least one partner keeping a foot out or at least pointed toward the door, obviously slacking in what was supposed to be an ironclad commitment to make it work. Partners may secretly start to blame and judge each other, often not accepting responsibility for their own role in whatever the circumstances are at the time. Some partners may overestimate their own role in the success of the company and begin to feel that they deserve the lion's share of compensation. (Remember Theodore, the hair stylist and Sandra, the operations manager?)

In some cases, one or all partners may begin to covertly consider getting out. At this stage of the game, one glance will make clear the strength or flimsiness of the commitment the partners have actually made. This is a crucial time to seek an objective expert to facilitate the conversations and help bring about resolutions before it's too late. Saving the partnership might not be the optimum outcome, but ending it in a way that is a win for everyone should be the goal.

Most of us would rather not argue or talk about subjects that push our emotional buttons. Dr. Dean Ornish, award winning cardiologist and author of six books, including *Stress, Diet & Your Heart: A Lifetime Program for Healing Your*

DOI 10.1515/9781547400188-013

Heart Without Drugs or Surgery, points to the stress that comes from conflict as the greatest cause of disease. While not necessarily one of the finer experiences in life, conflicts are inevitable and in business can be utilized as motivators for creating positive change. If you and/or your partner(s) find yourselves avoiding one another or not being completely transparent, it is a sign of some disagreement or contention that needs to be resolved. When disgruntled feelings turn into ongoing conflict, emotions override the issue, and thinking and speaking clearly about the situation may become impossible. Much the way laughter is contagious, so is conflict. While you and your partner(s) are mired in a stew of strife, employees, clients, vendors and family members—as well as the bottom line—all experience the trickle-down effect.

Avoidance was the coping mechanism used by Arnold and Craig, who co-owned three auto parts supply stores in the mid-western United States. Conflict caused them to avoid each other like the plague. Arnold believed he was doing most of the work and that his level of compensation should reflect that, while Craig vehemently disagreed. They each focused on their area of expertise. Arnold visited each store twice a month to oversee operations and was also in charge of the team of managers and marketing. Craig was in charge of the finances and vendor relationships. Neither grasped how their focus on the business had eroded due to their lack of collaboration.

Since Arnold and Craig didn't meet regularly, meetings with the management team were often skipped and coordination between divisions was not happening. No one was looking at the big picture and how this lack of communication was impacting the business. At every level, people were feeling demoralized and some of the most valuable employees began circulating their resumés to other companies. The business was in danger because those running it had failed to resolve their conflicts.

A friend suggested to Craig that he call me. Since my policy is to work with partners together, Craig had to convince Arnold to get on at least one call. Our coaching lasted for four months. It began with me guiding them in how to listen to each other. At the end of our first hour session, they were grateful and amazed that they could have a calm conversation without strong emotions taking over. That first session brought them to the realization that their basic original desires and dreams for this business remained.

They also realized that they actually still liked each other and began to understand that the resentment each harbored toward the other was the result of not communicating. Each was doing what he thought he should, but they had begun to travel separate paths. They were ignoring some of the greatest advantages of having a partner by no longer brainstorming together or sharing responsibility. Once we hit on the root cause of their conflict, they were able to get back on track to move their business in a positive direction.

In the subsequent three months of coaching, they were able to see how this dispute had played havoc with and endangered the success of the business. With renewed commitment to making it work, they agreed to institute a strategy of regularly structured meetings, each with a purposeful agenda. Putting all of this in place and with a new level of commitment, their staff felt the newly positive atmosphere, which was reflected in a more robust bottom line.

ESSENTIAL QUESTIONS: *Have you ever or do you now have something that makes you so angry that you avoid speaking about it to another person? Can you now see how that may be causing harm to you, the other person, your relationship and others tangentially? Are you willing to approach this person in good will and let them know you would like to resolve it? Would you be willing to get help to facilitate the conversation, if needed?*

Red Flags That Your Business Partnership is in Jeopardy

What are the signs that indicate your partnership relationship is potentially in trouble? If you've vetted each other well at the outset, you should be on the same page about most everything—most importantly, core values, goals, ethics, trust and overall ability to communicate honestly. Sometimes, though, even in the best of circumstances, things change for one or more of the partners. For example, at the start you and your partner(s) agreed to adopt a slow growth policy, taking minimal financial risks. After a short period of time, one partner decides that more aggressive growth and risk taking would be desirable. Neither of you is able to convince the other of your respective viewpoints, and now a stalemate is causing tension. The partner who wants this change is thinking of leaving, but hasn't voiced it yet. As a result, you are avoiding each other and the downward spiral has begun.

Another scenario is when one partner begins to slack off or overwork. The other partner(s) either must pick up the slack or be concerned about the work-life balance of the workaholic. Talking about it could allay concerns and clarify what is expected of each; but it may not, and then again the downward spiral may be triggered.

A change in vision is no small issue and can be very challenging when it occurs. Having been on the same page at the outset, when one partner has a change of heart and the partners' perspectives are different about some aspect of the original vision, the business could derail altogether. The vision keeps the business on track. Every policy and procedure should reflect it. Taking a direction different from the one you committed to in the first place reminds me of my ballroom dance instructor who told me, "When your feet point in two different directions, you have to choose one." Clearly the vision of the partners must be in alignment. If changes are worth considering, then take the time to communicate until it is resolved and agreed upon.

Imagine Zappos or Apple having their core values regarding customer service or employee benefits challenged. Changes in the way they treat either of these populations could vastly affect their reputation, the way they do business and ultimately the success of the business itself. Your business may not be on the same scale as these two, but the same issue about core values being challenged by one partner and not agreed to by the others would have the same destructive effect.

Averting a Crisis

The best solution to conflict resolution is actually conflict prevention. It is best to resolve things at the disagreement level before they explode into full-on conflicts. This is more easily done with clearly written expectations, goals, and crisis management plans in place. If you have those in place, when a conflict arises you can always go to your business plan, together discussing where you have gone awry. The plan may no longer fit, but at least it can help you open the conversation and make necessary changes.

Now is the time to remember that you had good reasons for choosing your partner, if you were honest and sincere in your initial evaluation and desire to succeed. Keeping that in mind when things get rough will help smooth the waters. Reminding yourself of your partner's positive attributes that led you to enter into this partnership in the first place will help you find your way back to that place of harmony and mutual respect.

To avert a crisis, consider doing the following:
– Have resources available: an emergency fund, a designated coach or other consultants dealing with specifics like technical needs, key employees who can step in, alternate sources of income and refined communication skills.
– Hold regular meetings to recognize, discuss and preempt problem areas before they erupt. I cannot stress this enough.
– If the crisis is totally unexpected, the partners, rather than attacking each other, should count on their commitment to the success of the partnership then pull together and handle it.

- Ask for help from an expert. If necessary, call in a coach/consultant to facilitate difficult conversations.
- When in sessions with your coach, acknowledge that your way is not the only way. Get comfortable devising a solution that is a win-win for everyone.
- Open your mind and keep your emotions in check when working through conflicts so that you will have a clearer thought process and greater patience.

A successful business is not just your livelihood, but likely one of the biggest parts of your life—providing for your family, creating jobs for your employees, offering a good product or service to your customers and being an asset to your community. Think of the far-reaching scope of your business when you are tempted to avoid dealing with conflicts. I can't emphasize enough that your conflict prevention and resolution skills greatly impact all of those involved in the business, not just you and your partner.

TIP: We've focused on listening skills in the last chapter but I cannot stress enough that listening is the most important skill in knowing how to communicate in order to prevent and resolve conflicts.

An Exception to the Rule

As much as I am an advocate of discussing disagreements or bad feelings as they occur, there is one circumstance under which I suggest you wait before addressing your concerns; that is, when your partner (or anyone) does something to push your buttons and send you into an emotional state. If you aren't able to talk in a calm manner, give it a day or two until you can do these things:

1. Calmly describe to yourself the event as it happened. Go over it and, if it helps, write it down in detail, as if it is a report.
2. With a commitment to being honest, ask yourself if you had some level of responsibility in what happened. Seeing that you played a part in it, you may conclude that it's no big deal.
3. If you did or didn't play a role, evaluate the effect it is having on you and your relationship.
4. When you can be calm, talk about it until it is resolved. Do not keep it to yourself if you feel that a resolution is needed.

How Business Partners Might Manage a Crisis . . .but Shouldn't
- Attack and blame
- Take to drink or other substances
- Disappear and avoid
- Pass the buck
- Become hysterical
- Project your anxiety or anger onto others
- Take it out on your spouse or other loved ones

When a Conflict Erupts

If tensions have heated up to the point of an outburst, follow these tried-and-true ways to handle the situation:
- Remain calm
- Analyze the situation
- Review former successful resolutions
- Evaluate the repercussions of the crisis
- Check your "what if" scenario plans
- Examine options
- Break down the required actions to small tasks
- Delegate
- Confer with others
- Brainstorm for creative ideas with key players
- Accept responsibility
- Ask for help

***

Following the advice in this chapter—long before disagreements arise—will go a long way in helping your partnership become one in the 30% of partnerships that succeed. If you need more incentive to be proactive, consider all of the people who are affected by your partnership. You are becoming one of the small to mid-size businesses (SMEs) that creates employment and a cycle of spending in the community where you are located and beyond.

So my parting advice is to choose each other well, discuss all of the points in the BPAT (including your conflict resolution plan and exit strategy), and write your decisions clearly in the BPAT, as well as in your partnership agreement and business plan. Then commit to continuing the conversation forever in regularly scheduled meetings, using your best communication skills throughout. If you take all of these steps and are sincere in wanting to do what's best for your business, you will be well on your way to business partnership success.

Part IV: **Collaborations Is the New Currency**

Chapter 14
A Word About Joint Ventures

"Businesses once grew by one of two ways: grass roots up or by acquisition. Today, businesses grow through alliances—all kinds of dangerous alliances, joint ventures, and customer partnering—which, by the way, very few people understand."

–Peter F. Drucker,
management consultant, author, professor

You may be wondering why I am adding a special chapter exclusively about joint ventures. The subject of joint ventures is enormous and could easily fill a few bookshelves in any business library. For the purpose of this book, rather than going into depth about the subject, I've chosen to briefly pay homage to joint ventures because they're an important part of a growing trend towards collaborative partnerships. Joint ventures are partnerships between businesses rather than individuals, but in the end it's all the same, since businesses are comprised of individuals. In keeping with the content of this book, the discussion here will be limited to small business joint ventures, rather than the complications surrounding large corporate joint ventures.

You may have heard it said that collaboration is the new currency. Collaboration is fast replacing competition between many businesses that believe they can get more done together than by working alone. As I indicated right up front in Chapter 1, this is one of the top benefits to having a partnership. True, competition will always be a part of our free enterprise system, but it's refreshing to see that companies that were once fixated on how they could gain advantage from another's loss are now instinctively looking to see how they can benefit from another's gain by supporting it. I'm all for that and I hope you are, too. The trend toward working together is a worthy one, and it's redefining the face of commerce—not just in the United States but internationally.

Collaboration is an excellent way for businesses—both for profit and non-profit—to maximize goods and services to their clients, enter new market space and gain a higher return on investments for the owners, thus helping to stay ahead in a competitive field. For these reasons and more, we hear of joint ventures as an increasingly popular way to structure a business and accomplish more. There are many original, creative prototypes of joint ventures that are limited only by the imaginations, dedication and vision of their owners. Some are quite complex and involve large corporations, states, even countries, with both online and offline communities. As such, the meaning of the term "joint venture" varies depending on who is defining it. With some, the joint venture partners may

DOI 10.1515/9781547400188-014

actually share a physical space or equipment, such as trainers in a gym. Others may be able to take advantage of increased technological, operational or financial capabilities through a joint venture. In many cases, joint ventures allow entities to promote each other's complementary services or products, thereby adding value to their respective clientele while expanding market share. Take, for instance, the joint venture between the City of Tampa, Florida and Copa Airlines of Panama. Their mutual goal was clearly defined: to increase business between Panama and Tampa Bay. A smaller, more local example of a joint venture is the one between Jack Rutberg of Jack Rutberg Fine Arts, Inc., a renowned art gallery in Los Angeles, and restaurant owner M.D. Sweeney. Rutberg offers coupons that his gallery patrons can take to Sweeney's acclaimed Amalfi Restaurant and Bar. Sweeney then gives all coupon holders a discount on their dinner tabs. As a result, the two businesses are supporting each other and increasing traffic to both of them.

With all of the potential for good, there is bad news: joint ventures of all sizes are failing at the same 70% rate as the rest of business partnerships and for many of the same reasons. The legendary founder of Panasonic, Konosuke Matsushita said it best: "Business is people." And as you already know because you've been reading this book, it's all about the relationships and the communication between the people who run the businesses.

The big difference between a business owned by partners or co-founders and a joint venture partnership is that in a JV there are more complexities because there are more moving parts already in motion with their own way of doing things. As with any business collaboration, problems can arise when there is a lack of clarity about these moving parts—such as, who actually is leading, what are the tasks and who is responsible for carrying them out, differences in culture, poor integration processes of the two separate and distinct entities, how monies will be collected and distributed, and who owns which assets. All of these issues, especially when added to the usual ones between individuals (like those discussed throughout this book), constitute areas of vulnerability and can affect decision-making, misalignment in visions and missions, operations policies and management styles. When established companies don't address these things effectively, the high failure rate is no surprise.

For these reasons, it's essential to discuss, decide and write your business plan and joint venture partnership agreement in detail. In many cases, such details are taken for granted and discussed just briefly if at all, thus making the joint venture road a bumpy one. For the same reasons I wrote the BPAT, I have also written a Joint Venture Agreement Template for small and mid-size businesses to guide owners through the necessary discussions to clarify and document the decisions they make. Just as in a business partnership, the most important thing is to find out about each other and your respective businesses in terms of character, core values, reputation, personality, shared values, goals and work styles. This, in effect, is the dating phase of the joint venture. In putting your deal together, work through how the project will be launched, which business will be responsible for marketing, and how monies will be collected and distributed, as well as the requirements in terms of people and technology needs. Take care not to make assumptions or take anything for granted.

Collaborations for a Cause

"I am of the opinion that my life belongs to the whole community, and as long as I live it is my privilege to do for it whatever I can."

–George Bernard Shaw

One joint venture of a slightly different nature is the growing trend of businesses to align themselves with a nonprofit organization, a cause of some kind, or a community initiative. In doing so, the nonprofit gains funds and possibly expertise and volunteer time from employees, as well as a larger support base. In turn, the business expands its market reach to new customers who care about and support the cause and/or the community. The company may also benefit from political support, public acknowledgment and, of course, tax credits. One local example that I recently read about was how Thrive Furniture donated more than $10,000 worth of furniture to Los Feliz Charter School for the Arts (LFSCA), located in the Eastside of Los Angeles.

In forming your business partnership and devising your mission/vision statements, take time to contemplate initiatives and projects through which your company—based on its core values—can give back to the community. More and more businesses are adopting a triple-bottom-line business model and doing this as a matter of course. Think of TOMS Shoes, LLC, for example, founded in 2006 by Blake Mycoskie. Their "One for One" model matches every pair of shoes purchased with a pair of new shoes for a child in need. While TOMS is an LLC and not a partnership, collaboration is so foundational to their operations that they've hired a Chief Giving Officer and built a team of 20 individuals dedicated to every aspect of giving. This team oversees a variety of joint ventures and other collaborations with villages, other nonprofits and organizations around the world.

Another good "for profit" example is Starbucks, voted the 2014 World's Most Ethical Company by the Ethisphere Institute. Although Starbucks's corporate vision has always been to redefine the coffee drinking experience for everyone around the world, their mission is to inspire and nurture the human spirit—one person, one cup and one neighborhood at a time. To fulfill this mission, Starbucks has initiated a great number of collaborations with businesses and communities around the globe that have helped to define how the company sources its products, invests in communities and minimizes its environmental footprint.

These are two well-known examples of companies that are making a difference in the world through the spirit of collaboration. They demonstrate what is possible—on a small, community based scale, as well as globally—and their lead has helped to inspire many small business owners, as well. But remember that whether or not you decide to align your business with a nonprofit, your community is greatly enhanced by the success of your business. Always take into account the ripple effect that your partnership has when you are making decisions on a daily, monthly and yearly basis.

If you decide to form a joint venture, I advise you not to view it as just a casual project. Perform the same due diligence that you would when forming a business partnership. Choose your partners carefully. Get to know their owners intimately. Communicate with transparency in order to build trust and mutual respect. And think collaboratively! This "new currency" has an immeasurably high value because at its core is the desire to create a win-win for all parties involved.

Chapter 15
Parting Thoughts on Partnerships

"And trust me not at all, or all in all."

–Alfred Lord Tennyson, "The Idylls of the King"

As you may have surmised by now, I am determined to help bring about more business partnership successes—not just for the partners involved but also their families, communities and industries, both locally and globally. I've written this book from my heart in order to help guide you to success and thereby have you join me in reversing the abhorrent 70% partnership failure statistic.

You've read about successful partnerships, some failed ones and others that turned their downward spiral up again. Key essentials are shared by all of them. In the successful ones, *trust* was talked about first and foremost; in the ones that fizzled or flopped altogether, trust was eroded.

Next are *respect* and *willingness* to do whatever the businesses need to have done without the partners counting the hours and minutes they put in. We also see in these partners' stories a readiness to be *transparent*, make solid *commitments*, then take full *responsibility* for knowing the big picture of the business overall—including decisions that aren't in their direct line of job responsibilities.

If the individuals are in business with a relative, friend or spouse, the successful partners set *boundaries* between personal and business life, and stick to them.

Finally, and of utmost importance, the most essential key to successful partnerships is *communication*. Keep the *conversations* going and schedule them in on a regular basis. Hold meetings in which you plan, evaluate, tell each other what annoyances or disagreements you have, then talk about them until everything is resolved. Successful partners *do not avoid each other* in order not to face resentment. Note that all the successful partners discussed in this book talked about arriving at *consensus* and agreed not to do anything without it.

Essentials to Your Partnership Success: A Summary

First and foremost, it is essential to *choose the right partner*. You've been given a guide and stories to illustrate how to do it effectively. Do not ever want the business so badly that you ignore red flags or rush into it before you know each other well enough and your trust is rock solid.

DOI 10.1515/9781547001088-015

After choosing the right partner, next comes the decision making process and recording those decisions into the BPAT to further solidify your relationship and eliminate all misunderstandings about who is doing what. Your *values, vision* and *mission statements* are crucial. Use them to guide the way you do business.

Conflict prevention is better than *conflict resolution*, but have a plan in place to deal with it. Equally essential is having an *exit strategy*. Start with the picture of where you would like to end up. What will you put in place if something happens other than what you planned? Talk about preparations for all *unexpected scenarios* and have plans in writing, knowing that they will likely change but at least you have a starting point.

Following your completion of the BPAT, take your decisions to a lawyer to draw up a *partnership agreement,* including some of the legalities that are necessary.

Using all of the information you have decided upon, move into creating a living *business plan*. Use its fluidity to modify or change as you move along, always evaluating how the plan is working.

★★★

A Final Note Before I Leave You to Your Business Partnership

I have no aspirations to be a professional author but this book had to be written. I find it intolerable that such a vital aspect of the lives of individuals—all members of the local and global economy—should fail. People have dreams and a desire to prosper. We need jobs or a means of livelihood. We yearn for a sense of community belonging, and have a strong innate propulsion to take good care of our families and loved ones as best we can. More of us are also feeling called to give back to others in some way.

So when I speak about business partnerships, I'm speaking about everything. These relationships permeate everything. My goal in writing a step-by-step guide about how to actually do a partnership—from the point of considering it to living it day in and day out—has been to give you everything you need to make it work, because, if it does not, the repercussions are practically immeasurable in their potential destruction.

I've said it several times, yet it bears repeating one last time: in forming your partnership, or even in considering ending it, a lot of people beyond the partners will be deeply affected by the outcomes. Keep everyone in mind as much as possible when making your decisions and commitments.

Thank you for taking the time to read *Business Partnership Essentials*. I would love to hear from you about what you've learned and what you are up to regarding your partnership. If you have comments or questions, feel free to email me directly at dl@bizpartnerpro.com. I offer you my heartfelt support for a successful partnership relationship through which you flourish and thrive beyond your wildest dreams.

Appendix A
Keys to Effectively Delegating and Having Time for Yourself

You probably know that delegating work to others is a great and appropriate way to save time, prioritize your own agenda and to focus on what you prefer to be doing. The key is to know when and how to delegate well. It's not just a matter of handing some work over to another person to do it.

What gets in the way of successful delegation? Here are a few common factors:
– You have not taken the time to analyze all you are doing and therefore do not have the awareness of what you could delegate.
– You prefer to be in control and feel the need to do it all yourself.
– You do not have the confidence that anyone else could do it well enough.
– You enjoy doing it and don't want to give it up.
– You may feel that you will not be able to justify the time you have opened up for yourself.

If you are having trouble getting past some of these, engage someone (a coach, therapist, colleague) to help you.

Eight Keys to Successful Delegation

Delegation is a key to successfully making sure that work gets accomplished effectively. However, if you do not do it right, the result will just create more problems. Here are the keys to making it work:
1. Take the time to look at everything you are doing. Make a list not only of the big projects, but break down the small details; for example, phone calls that need to be made, research to be done, whatever it is. Indicate with check marks or create three separate lists for 1) those that could be done by someone else, 2) what you'd like to get rid of if you could, even if the how is not obvious, and 3) the things you really must or want to keep for yourself.
2. Identify the likeliest person to do those tasks you want to delegate. Make sure that they are capable of doing them and are not on overload themselves.
3. Even if you are their boss, engage them politely by asking if they are okay with it. Do they have the time and resources to do it? If they are too burdened at the moment? If so, when will they be in a position to take it on? When you

DOI 10.1515/9781547400188-016

show respect for people, they will be inclined to help out. Of course, as boss you have the right to insist, but you'd be wise to do it with respect and appreciation.

4. Make sure the person you choose is capable to do the task successfully. If not, you are setting someone up to fail and yourself to be even more stressed.

5. Communication is key. Many people fall short here. You need to have a clear picture of the outcome you want and communicate it clearly to the person who will do it. Often we assume that the other person knows—when, in fact, because they are creative in their own way, they may produce a very different outcome than the one you envision.

6. Think through the degree of difficulty of this task and if it is not simple; make a plan that has step after step. Explain to the person who will be doing the task why it needs to be done a certain way by a certain time. Build in check-in points and a timeline to meet deadlines.

7. Overall, keep these points in mind:
   - Assess each task regarding the appropriateness to delegate.
   - Who would be the best person to ask to do it?
   - Make sure you are very clear in communicating how and what you want.
   - What measures will you use regarding deadlines and quality of work?
   - Remember to express respect and appreciation for the person helping you.

8. Now that you've relinquished the task, use the time wisely; prioritize everything you are doing and don't forget to schedule time for some downtime on your priority list.

Appendix B
Business Partnership Success Meter

Welcome to your Business Partnership Success Free Assessment!

Take the assessment below. Consider each question as it relates to your current or future business partnership. Following the assessment is your Success Meter...how successful is your partnership? Don't peek before you're done.

Let's get started! Simply answer yes (Y) or no (N).
1. My partner and I trust each other.
    Y   N
    My partner and I have a relationship with each other outside of business.
    Y   N
2. This business is an equally high priority for both my partner and I.
    Y   N
3. My partner and I are putting together or—already have a professional team of experts (lawyer, CPA, insurance agent, contractor, etc) that are knowledgeable, trustworthy and accessible.
    Y   N
4. My partner and I agree on the vision, purpose and long term goals of the business.
    Y   N
5. My partner and I talk regularly about everything that causes tension between the two of us and arrive at a win/win resolution.
    Y   N
6. My partner and I have a plan to solve disagreements regarding the business in a win/win manner.
    Y   N
7. My partner and I have discussed various exit strategies depending on life or market events.
    Y   N
8. My partner and I agree on the degree of risk to take financially.
    Y   N
9. My partner and I like each other.
    Y   N
10. My partner and I each have a clear job description.
    Y   N

DOI 10.1515/9781547400188-017

Success Meter Scores

Total your Yes (Y) answers to determine your place on the scale below:

0-4: Find another partner or get help to work on turning more answers into yes!

5-8: You are only half way there. How do you get to the next level?

9-11: Congratulations! You are well on the way to success. Keep building on what is working

Congratulations! You have successfully completed the assessment. How did you do? Are you and your business partner on the road to success or destruction?

Thank you for taking this assessment. It is my goal to help as much as possible for your partnership to succeed.

I have interviewed many entrepreneurs in partnerships and some professionals and experts who work with them in the last few years, and realized that most of them know very little about creating the groundwork for a successful long term business relationship. In fact, many of them didn't realize how worthwhile it could be to do it right in the beginning and prevent the necessity of having to learn hard lessons in hindsight.

Don't be among those who skip the steps and pay a high price for it later. Let me guide you, whether you are in startup position or already well into your business with a partner there is much that can be done to make things better.

My best wishes for your success,
Dorene

Dorene Lehavi, MSW, PhD
dl@dorenelehaviphd.com
323-931-7204
www.dorenelehavi.com

Index